Psychodynamics

*Beyond Demographics
and Psychographics*

Psychodynamics

*Beyond Demographics
and Psychographics*

The New Key to Understanding
Target Marketing and Matchmaking

John Tyler

Published by KBPublishing House
333 E 14th Street, Suite 3C
New York, NY 10003

Manufactured in the United States of America, or in the United Kingdom when
distributed elsewhere.

Tyler, John
Psychodynamics: Beyond Demographics and Psychographics

ISBN:
    paperback: 978-1-938015-24-3
    eBook: 978-1-938015-25-0

Cover Design: Scribe
Interior Design: Scribe

www.psychodynamics.com

Contents

Foreword

Just what we need, right? Yet another book on who we are and what makes us tick. But at least it's a new way of thinking that hasn't been done to death before. As a matter of fact, it hasn't been done at all before.

This isn't a how-to book. It probably isn't even a self-help book. It is essentially a *new way* of looking at and thinking about people. No, it is not a book about demographics. And it's not a book that repackages demographic descriptions and gives them fanciful marketing names ("soccer moms," "upwardly mobile SUV drivers," etc.). It's not even a book about "psychographics"—which according to *A Dictionary of Marketing Research* by Audits and Surveys, Inc., is "a description of groups which goes beyond demographic characteristics to *include attitudinal variables*."

What it is, then, is a book about psychodynamics. (Hold on! Before you decide this book is a primer on criminal behavior, let us hasten to point out that "psychodynamics" does not refer to the actions of an energetic psychotic person.) According to Merriam-Webster Dictionary, the principal definitions of psychodynamics are "motivational forces acting especially at the unconscious level" and the "explanation or interpretation (as of behavior or of mental states) in terms of mental or emotional forces or processes."

Can we sharpen that meaning? What we have attempted to do in this book is to describe the American populace in the context of shared: values, convictions, ideals, morals, attitudes, beliefs, motivations, and mental states—whether consciously or unconsciously adopted—independent of age, income, education, and other demographic categories routinely measured by the census.

What we found over the course of a study process that interviewed more than 10,000 Americans in depth was that there are eight distinct psychodynamic types of Americans. Individuals within each of these types inherently get along best with others of the same type and in varying degree with the other seven types. We call them *psychodynamic types*.

This book describes who these types are, how we discovered them, and what they are like.

What is the significance of any of this? It may prove to be a way to help people identify and connect with others with whom they are most likely to be compatible. And it might just get people to think about themselves more objectively by pointing out that they are a combination of strengths and weaknesses that are unique and distinct from seven other types of Americans. It may clear up some of the reasons why some people get along with some people and not so well with others. It may call to mind some of the encounters they have had with others that went either swimmingly or not so well. In sum, it may lead them to reconsider how they might get along better and/or more tolerantly with others.

Acknowledgments

"I have known Jack for over 20 years. Jack Tyler is years ahead of most marketers and teaches companies how to look at the market differently and more profitably. Jack knew demographics had little value over 20 years ago and has been showing companies better ways to market ever since. The clients that work with Jack and his psychodynamics segmentation strategy have a huge competitive advantage that shows up in sales. His book gives you the insight on how to get started in your own company."

DR. TIMOTHY MANTZ,
Dean School of Business,
Asssociate Dean of the Graduate School,
Keiser University

Dr. Thomas Piazza, associate director, Survey Research Center, University of California at Berkeley, has provided and continues to provide understanding, technical assistance, support, and friendship over the years.

Greg Harmon, director of custom research, Borrell Associates, has been an invaluable friend and supporter from the beginning of our development of psychodynamics. As he has said, "Since Arnold Mitchell's pioneering book *The Nine American Lifestyles* came out and the concept of psychographics conquered the marketing and advertising worlds, and with the advent of the social media and Amazon's pioneering work in 'behavioral profiling,' a real need has emerged for understanding audiences at a similar level of sharpness. Tyler's groundbreaking work in developing an analytic model that does not depend on respondent demographics at all makes psychodynamics a real step forward."

Lynne Bergherm Tyler has been my patient and talented helpmate throughout the writing process and has contributed extraordinarily both in the thinking and writing of this book.

Introduction

Connecting With the

Eight Psychodynamic Types

Why do we connect easily with some people and not with others? The crux of this book is about "connecting"—which we are defining as relating to other people in terms of the strength of the shared values, beliefs, convictions, attitudes, and motivations that we believe are key to mutual affinity.

Our research has revealed that there are 8 separate and distinct types of Americans, based on their similarities and differences on more than 50 psychological and sociological factors intrinsic to (1) their motivations, beliefs, and deeply held convictions; (2) the nature and strength of their connectedness to others; and (3) the strength of their connection to various aspects of the American culture.

This book explains the eight types; their detailed natures; and the who, what, why, and where of how well people of a particular type connect with the other types. It describes the reasons for differing levels of affinity among the eight types. Some of the types connect immediately and well. Others connect less successfully or hardly at all. Some types connect well initially but do less well over time—sometimes because of a person's evolution from one type to another.

Defining people in the manner described in this book is different from the usual reliance upon factors such as (1) demography (age, income, education, etc.) or (2) common avocational interests (fishing, water skiing, Bible reading, casino gambling, etc.).

This system is the outgrowth of a research process whose original motivation was to develop a new marketing segmentation system that would help marketers and advertisers better understand and identify potential consumers for their products and services. But in the process of creating that system, we discovered what we believe to be considerably more valuable—a way of thinking that helps us better understand ourselves in relationship to others and some of the important reasons why we do or do not get along.

This book will help readers (1) understand themselves better by helping them determine which of the types they are, (2) sharpen their sensitivities toward others, (3) better understand how harmoniously their own characteristics mesh with those of other types, and (4) better identify and connect with the people with whom they are likely to be most compatible.

I

The Early Going

The Journey of Discovery

EARLY DEVELOPMENT

Introduction

There are many points of view about what constitutes Americanism, and there are many "languages" used to define different types of Americans. We are accustomed to hearing different types of Americans described in any number of ways.

America is a diverse culture, the result of an agglomeration and evolution of values, attitudes, and beliefs from many cultures over a period encompassing the last several hundred years.

Some like to think of Americanism in terms of the Statue of Liberty alchemy—a transformation of the ingredients from huddled masses and teeming refuse from other cultures into the refined gold of the American culture.

Others like to think of Americanism as reflected by a stable set of values and beliefs anchored in the eighteenth century.

The founding fathers made sure that we would not escape self-examination by instituting the census and making it law that it would be repeated every 10 years. And the census has fostered our fascination with self-examination and self-description by continuingly adding new ways for us to categorize ourselves. Currently, the census measures U.S. households/persons in terms of the following characteristics/demographic variables, among others:

Gender
Age
Income
Education
Marital status
Ethnicity
Home ownership
Area type of residence (urban, suburban, rural)
Geographic location of residence

Private firms now purchase this information, manipulate it, and re-package it in various ways for sale to interested parties, including professional marketers who use it to identify and locate target audiences.

Thinking about people in terms of demographic perspectives is now commonplace. The layperson is accustomed to think of himself or herself and others in terms of demographic descriptors. And marketers have gotten people so accustomed to the process that the layperson now not only understands how demographics are used in marketing but also is accustomed to thinking of himself or herself in terms of his or her relationship to "target market profiles"—mixes of specific demographic characteristics that indicate those sectors of the populace with a statistically greater-than-average predisposition to buy something or to do something.

For example, demographic analysis might reveal that the target market profile for a new type of antibacterial hand-cleaning product consists of females ages 25–44, college graduates, homeowners, and households with an annual income of $50,000 or more. And then, having described their target market in that fashion, marketers and advertisers then go on to try to predicate their efforts to appeal to, to reach, and to influence people of that profile (and others) to buy the product.

As someone who has been involved with this process for a considerable length of time, it has always been our point of view that demographic understanding was important, but only one part of the puzzle.

In a memorable and insightful cartoon, there was a middle-age advertising professional bemusedly explaining to a visitor, "I know that half of my advertising budget is wasted—the problem is I don't know which half."

Demographic data has long been the linchpin of marketers' efforts. A simple way of defining marketing strategy/tactics is to say that its function is *to identify, reach, and influence target markets.*

Identification of target markets. "Target markets" have historically been defined by demographic elements—for example, female, age 25 to 44, college graduate, homeowner, annual income $50,000 or more. Target markets are usually defined by surveys of product users.

Reaching target markets. Analysts use the science of geodemographics to determine how well a geographic area contains concentration of the target profile and in deciding upon the optimum media mix in which to place advertising. Media specialists rely on the demographic profiles of each medium under consideration.

Influencing the target market is typically the responsibility of advertising agency "creative" people. It is their job to assess, create, and present the messages and format most likely to influence/motivate the target market in ways beneficial to the client. In this effort, they may be aided by surveys, focus groups, and other formal and informal means of understanding the motivations of the (demographically defined) target market. However, demographics are usually of limited utility in this regard.

Geodemographic systems use combinations of demographically defined census information within a certain geographic area to assign people into one or another of roughly 40 to 50 "types" (called such things as "blue blood estates," "inner city ghetto dwellers," etc.). These systems have included Prizm, Acorn, ClusterPlus, and others. These systems help identify geographic areas that offer concentrations of demographic target market segments for various types of consumer products and services.

PSYCHOGRAPHICS

Psychographics might be described as "a step up from demographics." According to *A Dictionary of Marketing Research* (published by Audits & Surveys, Inc., New York), psychographics is described as "a description of groups which goes beyond demographic characteristics to include psychological variables (e.g., personality traits)."

As typically used in the marketing community, psychographics usually means combining demographic and attitudinal variables into a categorization system that has a discrete number of "types."

Psychographic systems combine demographic information with some attitudinal information to categorize people into one of eight or nine "values and lifestyles" types. Such systems include the well-known VALS (Values, Attitudes, and Lifestyles) systems developed at SRI International (Stanford Research Institute) and various imitative or derivative systems. These systems have also frequently been used to understand and help segment the markets for consumer products and services as well as the media most effective in reaching these segments.

In our view, these systems are not terribly helpful in understanding the attitudinal, value, and motivational predispositions of the United States populace, although some of them purport to deal with these issues in that attitudes, motivations, and values are frequently conjectured or presumed as the probable or logical outcome of a particular set of demographic circumstances. To our knowledge, they are not based on large-scale, quantitative evaluation of the attitudinal characteristics presumed to be the case for a particular type-description.

In the case of values and lifestyles systems like VALS, which does not discourage its users from believing that these systems are attitudinally driven, the categorization process is highly influenced by the inclusion of demographics—age, income, education, and others—into the algorithm. For example, one of the original VALS system categories was "achiever," which was described as a person who has achieved high status in society as a result of success in business and who enjoys the material rewards associated with that success. However, a person was highly unlikely to be assigned to the "achiever" category unless he/she earned substantial income and was already in a managerial or administrative position. Nor was a person likely to be classified as a "survivor"—a materially disadvantaged person struggling with day-to-day survival—unless he/she was earning no more than a poverty-level income. In both examples, conclusions about the attitudinal makeup of the types were heavily influenced by the inclusion of demographic variables that biased the categorization in the directions that were purported to be attitudinal findings.

Understandably, psychographic systems have been criticized for being "demographically driven" (being no more effective than their demographic components alone), and it is true that combining demographic and attitudinal/psychological variables makes it difficult to assess the relative contribution and influence of the demographic variables versus the psychological ones.

Psychographics may come into pragmatic conflict with companies' preexisting systems of analysis and market planning—frequently based solely or heavily on demographics. Often there is no practical way to integrate the two ways of thinking.

Psychographic systems cannot be accurately modeled or predicted from demographics. Similarly, demographic modeling from psychographics is usually not effective.

Although the original motivation for this work was an attempt to develop a superior consumer values and lifestyle segmentation system, it took on a life of its own and a different perspective as it became apparent that the work had something significant to say about who we are as a people.

The system that we ultimately developed, which we are calling *psychodynamics*, set out to eliminate the weaknesses of previous systems, especially the psychographic ones, by totally eliminating demographics from the categorization and the description of various "types" of people.

Consequently, our typology can be considered a "pure" values and motivation system, one that is free from the influence of demographics.

Since the system is free of demographic influence, it can be used in concert with any demographic system or as an adjunct to those systems. However, it's greater benefit is probably in helping us better understand what really drives the thoughts and behaviors of contemporary Americans.

As this work began to take form, we realized more and more that it was crucial that we did not repeat the errors and the shortcomings of earlier systems. Although we were inspired and are highly indebted to the original VALS system, developed by Arnold Mitchell of SRI, and although VALS was a landmark exploration of Americans' values and lifestyles, it owed much of its structure to the personality development theories of Abraham Maslow, especially his notion of differing stages of personal development as life's basic needs become satisfied. Many people—ourselves included—found Mitchell's system a very easy to understand one and one that resonated in many ways with people's own insights into the types of people they encounter. However, Mitchell's system contained a condition that we wanted to avoid—the use of demographics as an integral and important part of the categorizing algorithm.

The psychodynamic system we will describe shortly is not a psychographic system because it *does not use demographics in any way* in categorizing or thinking about people. It is based totally on psychological/motivational considerations.

Psychodynamics is a target marketing alternative to demographics and psychographics. It is a typology developed over the past several years by means of extensive surveys and statistical analyses. It is a statistically accurate picture of eight types of people that compose the adult U.S. populace based on systematic differences in their values, beliefs, attitudes, convictions, and predispositions.

It is an attempt to help understand the motivational forces that lead us to behave the way we do, to provide insight into why we do or do not get along well with various other types of people, and to provide a benchmark understanding of the principal current mind-sets in the United States.

Psychodynamics is based wholly on people's attitudes, values, and behavioral predispositions. *Demographics are not used in any way in the algorithm* that categorizes people into one or another of the eight psychodynamic types. Because of this, it is very different from other systems, such as geodemographics or psychographics.

WHAT IS PSYCHODYNAMICS?

According to Merriam-Webster Dictionary, the word psychodynamics means (1) the "explanation or interpretation (as of behavior or of mental states) in terms of mental or emotional forces or processes," (2) the "motivational forces acting especially at the unconscious level," and (3) "the psychology of mental or emotional forces or processes developing especially in early childhood and their effects on behavior and mental states."

We are using the word in the context of the first and second meanings. In sum, psychodynamic segmentation refers to a system of categorizing people into types that is based wholly on psychological and motivational variables.

Benefits of the Psychodynamic Approach

Having no demographic components, psychodynamics can be used in the following ways:

As a powerful complement/addition to demographic understandings

As a stand-alone system of consumer insight and segmentation

The psychodynamic system we will describe is based on universal psychological characteristics (variables) that may well prove to be appropriate and applicable across countries and cultures.

Key Conceptual Criteria in Developing the Psychodynamic System

The following are several major conceptual objectives:

The approach must be clearly relevant as a way of identifying different sectors of the U.S. populace.

It must be operationally free of demographics.

The concepts and variables used in the investigation must encompass universal human characteristics to foster the possibility of the system's usefulness/application in cultures other than just the United States.

We decided that a combination sociological/psychological approach held the most promise. That approach offered the promise of accomplishing two separate but interrelated goals:

1. Sociologically—to segment the population according to the degree and strength of people's connectedness to their country
2. Psychologically—to define population segments on the basis of psychological difference and distance from one another

Again, if successful, this approach held the promise of the further benefit of segmentation applicability for countries/cultures other than the United States.

2

Benchmark Study of the American Cultural Center

STUDY OBJECTIVES

To begin, we needed to understand American values on a nationwide basis. There were two principal objectives to this study:

1. To determine what American values are. What core convictions, attitudes, beliefs, and predispositions define prototypical American values?
2. To determine the following:
    What groupings of people, if any, best represent different degrees of a common cultural connectedness?
    What characteristics distinguish one grouping from another?
    What is the psychological makeup of these groups?

HOW THE U.S. ADULT POPULACE RELATES TO ITS COUNTRY AND ITS CULTURE

Step 1 obtained a benchmark understanding of the attitudes of the nation as a whole in reference to these key issues. In developing that understanding, a large-scale, in-depth survey was used.

Variables Studied

Interview content was extensive. More than 50 motivational, attitudinal, and values-related dimensions and variables were studied, including the following:

Spirituality
Adherence to laws, rules, mores
Active/passive
Individualism
Self-centeredness
Connectedness to current institutions
Susceptibility to influence from outside/influence from within
Innovation/caution
Open-mindedness/closed-mindedness
Conventionality
Law abiding/law bending
Indulgence/restraint
Risk taking
Materialism
Excitement
Conventionality
Exhibitionism
Cultural expansiveness
Happiness with law enforcement
Frugality
Breadth of interests
Experimentation
Vigilantism
Learning
Self-gratification
Intellectualism
Leadership aspiration
Appropriateness of good manners
Fundamentalism
Xenophobia
Insularity
Nationalism

Preference for the known
Home centeredness
Stimulation seeking/avoidance
Local focus
Entitlement
Resistance to change
Trust in law enforcement
Pleasure in irritating others
Outdoors/indoors orientation
World perspective
Luxury focus
Confidence in institutions
Status consciousness/focus
Appearance focus
Rule bending
Tendency to live and let live
Contentment with status quo
Extravagance
Ego strength
Patriotism
Belief in/adherence to religious codes
Free-floating anger
Time-pressuredness
Self versus other orientation
Patience

Study Design

A nationally representative sample of 3,800 U.S. adults—balanced to parallel all demographic characteristics enumerated by the census—was the basis for this evaluation.

The interview procedure was an initial telephone contact to obtain respondent cooperation, and then an extensive questionnaire (with a monetary incentive) was mailed to the respondent's home, filled out, and mailed back.

Follow-up mailings to nonresponders were also accomplished. In all, a completion rate of 85% of initial contacts was realized.

The sample was poststratified to match the percentage distributions for the following U.S. demographic characteristics, as measured by the census:

Gender
Age
Annual household income
Education
Occupation
Marital status
Ethnic derivation
Home ownership/rental
Area of residence (urban, suburban, rural)
Different census region residence

Accuracy of the Findings

In total, 3,800 interviews were completed in this manner. This size sample is accurate to approximately 2% at the 95 in 100 confidence level. What this means is that, for an observed percentage result, the chances are approximately 95 in 100 that an observed percentage finding lies within 2% (plus or minus) from what would have been found had all U.S. adults been interviewed.

VALUES PROFILE OF THE U.S. ADULT POPULACE

Connectedness With the American Culture and Its Values

Americans' interests focus most strongly on their country and national developments, closely followed by interest in their local community and things affecting it and, at a lower level, on international concerns and developments.

Very substantial majorities of U.S. adults hold attitudes and convictions that bind them strongly to their country and its culture.

Americans identify strongly with their country, its values, and its institutions. Very strong majorities are patriotic; support U.S. positions and policy in reference to world affairs; and support a vigorous U.S. military, even in peacetime. Americans have little tolerance for other Americans who demonstrate against their country or foreign residents who are critical of this nation. Most Americans have a very local focus and feel closely connected to their local communities.

Support for the American Economy

Americans are strong supporters of the American economy, the free enterprise system, the American worker, and American products. Substantial majorities believe that their economic system of free enterprise is superior to all other systems, favor economic protectionism as a defense against other countries' growing economic power, and prefer to buy American products—but only if there is corresponding product quality and value. Americans' vacation and pleasure trip priorities center on their own country; Americans want to see America first.

Adherence to American Values, Laws, and Mores

Americans are law-abiding citizens and follow society's rules and conventions. They consider themselves conventional people and overwhelmingly say they obey prevailing laws, rules, and regulations. They lean toward the conservative rather than the liberal, although a large number consider themselves "middle-of-the-roaders."

Connectedness to the International Community

Even though Americans are strongly focused on their own country and its interests, they have significant curiosity and sensitivities about the larger world.

Substantial majorities of Americans are curious and open-minded about other countries. Although they believe that the United States behaves equitably in regards to the rights of other nations, they also believe that it is America's responsibility to behave less selfishly within the world community for the sake of a better world. Americans feel that it is *not* appropriate for our nation to be using such a disproportionate share of the world's natural resources. They believe that reductions in their own standard of living may be a consequence of these acts (but one they could accept) toward the goal of planetary survival.

In addition to their concern to the other peoples of the world, Americans have a strong concern about animals and favor additional efforts to guarantee their rights.

Americans' Sense of How Life Is Treating Them

Americans have a very positive view of the way life is treating them. The great majority of Americans believe that life treats them fairly and feel that they are coping successfully with life.

Spiritual/Religious/Moral Perspectives

Americans have a strong spiritual/religious/moral belief system and try to live within the precepts of their personal belief structure. They tend to be tolerant of other people who do not believe similarly to themselves.

Most Americans believe that God is a forgiving God and that there is not just one "true" religion. The great majority of Americans consider it very important to try to live their lives according to their religious and/or spiritual beliefs, and most people believe that their morals are higher than most others'. Christianity overwhelmingly has more appeal to Americans than Eastern religions. Most Americans believe in the Biblical story of God having created the world in a 6-day period. A third of Americans consider themselves born-again Christians. However, most Americans do not feel that people need to be religious in order to be good.

Virtually all Americans believe that the Golden Rule—"Do unto others as you would have them do unto you"—and the Old Testament's 10 Commandments are highly relevant and useful in today's society. Americans would like the federal government to take a hand in encouraging the practice of prayer in public schools.

Virtually all Americans believe in the practice of good manners as both highly relevant and important today. However, Americans are not without a perverse side to their natures. A small proportion readily admit to taking pleasure in irritating others, especially in small matters where they can be a hindrance to someone else's attempts to accomplish something.

Materialism

The majority of Americans are not materialistic. Americans almost universally reject the notion that "success in life" can be defined in materialistic terms and most are more oriented toward doing work they enjoy rather than on the monetary rewards of the job. Americans are not profligate spenders. Relatively few profess interest in buying expensive things just because they are expensive.

Personal Characteristics

Americans are very home oriented. They are, and try to be, conventional. They consider themselves to be healthy and energetic, are competitive, and are concerned about presenting a good physical appearance. They are lovers of the outdoors and outdoor activities.

Americans dislike being conspicuous. They much prefer to fit in with the group rather than stand out from it; they do not want to be perceived as outrageous. Although they drink alcoholic beverages, they are not in favor of marijuana being legalized (but more and more are leaning in that direction).

Psychological Characteristics

As a people, Americans have great forbearance, restraint, and tolerance. Relatively few have high levels of free-floating anger, indignation, or resentment (between 1 and 2 in 10 do, however).

Americans believe in fair play. Almost without exception, they do not expect special treatment and consideration or to be exempted from following society's rules.

Americans tend not to be pushy. They try to take other people into account in their day-to-day living and their general behavior. Twice as many say they would rather be taken advantage of than to take advantage of someone else.

Most Americans do not feel terribly time pressured, but about 3 in 10 do feel that they are always hurrying to try to get everything done that they are trying to accomplish.

The Role of the Sexes

The majority of Americans do not define women's fulfillment on the basis of being the centerpiece of a happy home. The notion that women should be relegated to the homemaker role is thought to be substantially out of date.

Sex-Related Issues

Americans believe that there is too much emphasis on sexual things in their culture and would like to see that influence lessened. Tolerance for homosexual behavior, same-sex marriages, and equal same-sex rights and privileges are consistently approaching majority status.

A majority of Americans have no objection to the federal government being involved in the funding of abortions.

Majorities of Americans believe there is too much sexual content on television and are opposed to the presence of pornographic movie theaters and bookstores. A majority believes that it is OK for an unmarried man or woman to have sexual relations.

Attitudes Toward Government Institutions and Big Business

Americans believe that politicians are generally corrupt and do not take an appropriately active role in helping with issues that Americans believe are important. Most Americans believe that politicians are bought off by private interests.

Americans believe that big business is too powerful and that business leaders do not have the interests of the average person at heart They strongly believe that there is too much power concentrated in the hands of big business and that America's business leaders are not doing enough to protect the economic interests of the average American worker.

Attitudes Toward Law Enforcement

Americans believe that governmental institutions generally are not successful in protecting the citizenry against criminals. Almost all Americans believe that too many criminals are avoiding punishment because of overly rigid protections of them that are built into our legal system. A majority believes that the police require additional power to do their jobs properly.

A relatively large minority feel that vigilantism is an appropriate response to inadequate processes of law.

Political Freedoms

Americans tend to want to deny government service opportunities to members of groups that have proven antagonistic to America.

Americans as Consumers

Americans much prefer to buy products with well-established brand names. They are brand focused and brand loyal. Once Americans have found a brand of product they like, they tend to stick with it.

Stability of Americans' Values and Belief Systems

Americans' values and belief systems are stable and resistant to change, The majority of Americans do not like change, are not risk takers, and believe that their personal value systems have remained relatively constant over the years.

3

Introduction to the Psychodynamic System

INTRODUCTION TO THE EIGHT PSYCHODYNAMIC TYPES

Detailed statistical analyses of the data led to the discovery of eight separate and distinct types of U.S. adults whose values, beliefs, and behavioral predispositions vary substantially in intensity and distance from a "perfect" representation of the American convictions, values, and attitudes mentioned in the previous chapter. People have a strong tendency to be just one of these eight types.*

THE EIGHT PSYCHODYNAMIC TYPES

The eight types are named according to one or more of the principal, identifying characteristics that compose their main motivational set. The values, convictions, and beliefs of four of the types tend to be most closely aligned (*congruent*) with the pattern of mainstream American values and beliefs, and four of them tend to be more distant (*divergent*) from those values and beliefs.

It is important for the reader to keep in mind that these eight types do not necessarily vary dramatically in values and beliefs from those of

---

* A small number are equally disposed to be more than one type.

the "typical" American pattern described in detail earlier. Rather, *the types should be thought of as stepwise departures from the center of American values and beliefs to a greater or lesser degree.*

The four *congruent* types are a closer fit with the values/belief patterns of the U.S. populace described earlier. They constitute a majority—55%—of the American adult populace. The four *divergent* types tend to have values/beliefs patterns that differ from that cultural core in degree and in various important ways. They constitute 45% of the U.S. adult populace.

And it is also important for the reader to keep in mind that *a person's predisposition to be one of the types is dynamic—not fixed or immutable—and is subject to change over time and with additional life experience.*

In general, in the following tables, the types are shown in decreasing order of harmony with the overall mainstream pattern of American values and beliefs.

The eight types have been named according to one or more of the principal, identifying characteristics that compose their main motivational predisposition or focus. The eight types and the estimated proportion of the U.S. adult populace each type represents are the following:

The Four Congruent Types—Totaling 55% of the U.S. Adult Populace

These types represent stronger relative congruence with the cultural connectedness factors described earlier.

    Mainstayers—20%
    Temperates—11%
    Doers—12%
    Aspirers—12%

The Four Divergent Types—Totaling 45% of the U.S. Adult Populace

These types represent relative degrees of divergence from the cultural connectedness factors described earlier.

    Empathizers—10%
    Enthusiasts—11%
    Nonconventionals—11%
    Explorers—13%

These eight groups of people are *true attitudinal types*, since the algorithm (statistical procedure by which people are categorized as one or another of the types) *includes no demographics.*

For this reason, readers accustomed to thinking about people on a demographic basis may find psychodynamics a useful independent way of thinking or as a helpful, clarifying addition to demographic categorization.

In addition to the extensive battery of values, beliefs, and attitudinal questions that were asked, comprehensive demographic questions were also asked. The subsequent analyses of the psychodynamics types determined that, within each type, there is substantial representation of people from *all subcategories* within the following demographic variables:

Gender
Age
Income
Education
Marital status
Ethnic derivation
Home ownership/rental
Area of residence (urban, suburban, rural)
Census region of residence

In addition to verifying that the eight types are true attitudinal types, this also means that the psychodynamics types *cannot be identified or modeled through combinations of demographic variables.*

The following table—"Factors Defining Comparative Levels of Connectedness to the Culture"—summarizes how each of the eight types varies in the degree to which it parallels mainstream American values, convictions, and beliefs in reference to five important cultural connectedness factors.

If the people composing a type do not differ appreciably from the U.S. adult populace as a whole on a factor, the table shows average ("Avg.") on that factor.

If a type scores higher on a factor, the table shows a plus sign ("+") or multiple plus signs to indicate various levels of increasing strength on that factor. The greater the number of plus signs, the greater the strength of the type on that factor.

If a type scores lower on a factor, the table shows a minus sign ("–") or multiple minus signs to indicate various levels of decreasing strength on that factor. The greater the number of minus signs, the lower the level of strength on that factor.

Factors Defining Comparative Levels of Connectedness to the Culture

	The four culturally congruent types				The four culturally divergent types			
	Main-stayers	Temperates	Doers	Aspirers	Empa-thizers	Enthusiasts	Noncon-ventionals	Explorers
% of U.S. population	20	11	12	12	10	11	11	13
Hold nationalistic beliefs/values	+++	++	+	Avg.	−	−	− −	+
Support their country/things of and by their country	+++	++	+	Avg.	Avg.	Avg.	− −	−
Adhere to its laws/rules/customs/mores	+++	++	+	+	Avg.	− −	− −	− −
Support patriotic events and activities	+++	+++	++++	−	− −	− − − −	− − − −	++
Receptive to ideas/influences from other countries/cultures*	− − − −	Avg.	−	Avg.	+++	Avg.	+	++++

* Note: A high score on this factor indicates less connectedness to the American culture.

PERSONAL FOUNDATIONS OF
CULTURAL CONNECTEDNESS

Further analyses of the data revealed that a person's connectedness to the American culture was also importantly related to a developmental, stepwise process of successful connections and relationships with various entities, as follows:

Contentment with one's self
Equitable relationships and dealings with other individuals
Living according to prevailing and understood spiritual and/or moral standards
Positive interaction and relationship with one's local community
Positive attitudes about the country and support for its interests

The following table ("Personal Foundations of Cultural Connectedness—A Developmental Perspective") shows that the four culturally congruent types (mainstayers, temperates, doers, and aspirers) match that pattern but in varying degree.

The four culturally divergent types depart from that pattern in various significant ways:

Empathizers are much like the congruent types on these factors but are less strongly connected to the country and less focused on its interests. Their principal pattern of conviction is that global concerns and issues are at least as important as their country's concerns and issues.

Enthusiasts and nonconventionals both score below average on happiness and contentment with one's self, treating other people fairly and equitably, having positive attitudes toward their local area/community, and having positive attitudes about their country and supporting its interests.

Nonconventionals, in addition, are the lowest of all eight types in the importance they attach to living in accordance with prevailing cultural spiritual/moral standards.

Explorers are a special case because they represent people who are in transition. Explorers are the only one of the types whose proportion in the population shows a relatively steady decline with advancing age. It appears that explorers transition into other types as they age—most likely becoming one of the four culturally congruent types. However, in most instances, explorers behave more like a divergent type than a congruent type.

Personal Foundations of Cultural Connectedness—A Developmental Perspective

	The four culturally congruent types				The four culturally divergent types			
	Main-stayers	Temperates	Doers	Aspirers	Empa-thizers	Enthusiasts	Noncon-ventionals	Explorers
% of U.S. population	20	11	12	12	10	11	11	13
Are happy/content with self	Avg.	Avg.	Avg.	Avg.	Avg.	– –	–	Avg.
Try to treat people as equal to oneself	+	++	Avg.	–	Avg.	– – –	– –	Avg.
Put high importance on living according to prevailing cultural spiritual/moral standards/codes	+	++	Avg.	+	Avg.	Avg.	– –	–
Have positive attitudes toward local area/local community	++	+	Avg.	Avg.	Avg.	– –	–	– –
Have positive attitudes about country and are focused on its interests	++	++	+	Avg.	–	–	– –	Avg.
Believe that global concerns/issues are at least as important as national concerns/issues*	– –	–	–	Avg.	+++	Avg.	Avg.	Avg.

* Note: A high plus score on this factor indicates *less* connectedness to the American culture.

4

Mainstayers

What Makes a Mainstayer?

CULTURAL CONNECTEDNESS

There is one type whose convictions, beliefs, values, and motivations are an almost perfect embodiment of cultural connectedness. For those reasons, we call them mainstayers. Mainstayers make up approximately 20% of the U.S. adult populace.

Mainstayers are a solid and stable core group of people with firm convictions. First and foremost, mainstayers consider themselves Americans. They are strong supporters of American ideas, interests, policies, actions, economy, and products. They personify the adage "My country, right or wrong."

They are the strongest possible advocates—although not necessarily the most vocal—of the American way of life and are quick to defend their country against people who might act against it or speak ill of it.

Their focus is primarily on things of concern within their own country, and they tend to be relatively uninterested in events or problems that occur outside of their national borders.

Mainstayers are strongly nationalistic. They support their country and its interests at every level and every opportunity. They believe in protecting their country from attempts at influence from abroad.

They believe that it is important for their country to have a strong and capable military, even in times of peace. Mainstayers tend to believe that military service is an important rite of passage for their country's young men.

They are highly moral people who place great importance in living according to high religious/spiritual/moral standards. Mainstayers pride themselves in adhering to American society's laws, rules, customs, and mores and have little tolerance for people who do not believe and behave similarly. They are passionate in their support of their country and tend not to think well of people who do not think and act similarly, either citizens or foreigners.

They believe that America tends to be inherently fair in its dealings with other nations and cultures and find it hard to imagine that America would ever behave unjustly toward another nation.

Mainstayers inherently believe that their country's interests should and do take precedence over the interests of competing cultures and over the interests of the world community in general.

Their priorities are much more oriented to experiencing their own country than any other cultures. They believe that their country has more sources of interest and pleasures than anyone could want— probably more than could be experienced in their lifetime. They want to get to know it thoroughly before considering visiting other countries. They do not expect that there would be much of interest or value to them originating from other countries/cultures.

They are highly resistant (the highest of all the types) to influences and ideas from other countries or cultures and have little interest in seeing or learning about other cultures. They want to "see America first."

They tend to be suspicious of foreigners and foreign ideas and tend to be less tolerant of non-American viewpoints, opinions, and practices. They believe that residency and citizenship should be reserved for people who truly value the opportunity. They are not strong supporters of free speech for people who they believe do not feel this way.

Mainstayers feel the need for better/more effective protective mechanisms for the national culture and its citizenry, especially in regard to a strong military; protection from foreign ideas and influences; protectionist policies that reference other countries' potential economic threat and dominance; containments against the power of big business; more effective legal, judicial, and law enforcement tools to combat criminals; eliminating corruption between politicians and special interests; making the government more responsive to the needs of the average person; and so on. In addition to feeling this strong connectedness with their country, they feel a similar, strong connectedness with the communities in which they live. They are not much interested in exploring options beyond the local. Happy and content with their ties and relationships to their local community and area, they have little interest in travel abroad or living abroad.

VALUES, ATTITUDES, AND MOTIVATIONAL MAKEUP

Mainstayers' focus is on their homes, their communities, and things that are close to home. Their preference is for the known and predictable rather than the new and the unknown. They are quite home centered and prefer quiet home occasions to going out to parties. They tend to consume little alcohol. They strongly prefer things that they know to things that are new to them. They like their lives to be regular, to be predictable, and to have a strong element of routine.

Mainstayers have strong, conservative religious beliefs. They are strongly committed to living in context with their precepts. Many mainstayers believe that their own particular religion is uniquely "true." They tend not to be very tolerant of other religions, belief structures, or people who are out of the cultural mainstream.

In general, they are temperate, nonmaterialistic people who value simplicity and simple pleasures and try to live their lives according to the culture's historic spiritual and moral guidelines.

They tend to avoid stimulants and do not wish to be or to be thought of as being drinkers, carousers, or libertines.

Mainstayers consider themselves conventional people. They believe strongly in the rule of law and in following the culture's prevailing laws, rules, and regulations. They favor conventional spiritual/religious orders and processes. They try to live according to a strict personal spiritual or moral code, frequently are active in organized mainstream religions, and tend to be unreceptive to religions/spiritual codes other than their own.

They value strongly the concept of rule and consider it highly important personally to stick to and to play by the rules.

They believe that it is wrong to take advantage of other people under any circumstances. They believe in the correctness and appropriateness of equal levels of consideration and privilege for all Americans and believe that it is wrong for anyone to seek special exemptions from the cultural rules, laws, and mores that were created for everyone to follow equally.

They view sex as a private experience appropriately restricted to marriage and as an inappropriate subject for entertainment and titillation. They have little tolerance for homosexuality and homosexual behavior.

They do not favor equal responsibilities for men and women and oppose legitimizing rights and privileges for same-sex couples. They believe that the traditional male and female roles—with the woman's primary focus on homemaking and caregiving—are appropriate and correct. They do not believe in strict equality between/among the sexes/genders and do not support the agendas of feminist interest groups.

Mainstayers do not consider the learning process to be fun. They tend to think that they have already accumulated enough practical information for their purposes.

Mainstayers dislike change, and their values and beliefs are by far the most stable/permanent of all the eight types. They prefer sticking to what they already know and enjoy. They do not easily give up the known and the liked for the new and the unknown.

They are predisposed to favor familiar brands and tend to be loyal to such brands for long periods of time. Mainstayers prefer familiar destinations and locations for their vacations and pleasure trips.

Overall, they are content with their status quo. They like what they do. Mainstayers tend to be happy and content. They feel that life treats them fairly and that they are coping successfully with life.

They enjoy watching television. They tend to be frugal and will not spend exorbitantly or impulsively to get what they want. They are not focused on self-gratification, self-indulgence, or luxury.

Mainstayers are not competitive people and do not care much whether they hold positions of leadership in the groups in which they are participants. Their preference is to blend in with the crowd. They do not like to be noticed or spotlighted and do not purposely do things that will draw attention to themselves.

Mainstayers do not consider themselves terribly physically fit. Neither are they much concerned about the personal physical image they present to the world.

Mainstayers do not much trust the behaviors or motivations of businesses or business leaders. They feel that these entities do not have sufficient concern for the economic well-being of the average person.

Mainstayers would favor stricter law enforcement. They believe that the legal system and people within the law enforcement profession are handicapped by not having adequate laws, processes, and tools to deal appropriately with people who are obvious wrongdoers. They would favor revisions to these circumstances that would better guarantee that criminals would actually get the punishment they deserve.

DEMOGRAPHIC TENDENCIES

There is substantial representation of mainstayers within all demographic categories and subgroups.

ACTIVITIES AND LIFESTYLES

Both mainstayers and temperates pursue very limited numbers of activities, hobbies, and avocations. They are tied for the lowest level of such activity among all the eight types. Their range of interests tends to be narrow, and they focus their energies on a relatively few things. Doing a small number of things repetitively does not bore them.

They do not care much for activities that involve risk and/or danger. They tend to be cautious and to play it safe. They prefer sure things to risk; they do not much like to gamble or take part in games of chance.

They are not avid outdoors people and do not much care for getting dirty. They tend to be somewhat squeamish. A backyard barbeque is much more preferable to a mainstayer than roughing it outdoors. They tend toward the peaceful and serene and are not much interested in activities oriented toward excitement and thrills.

Mainstayers' favorite activities and interests focus on their family, their home, their spiritual life, and their country and include the following:

Traveling in the United States
Walking for health

Home workshop/do it yourself
Gardening
Time with grandchildren
Crafts
Bible/devotional reading
Hunting
Sewing
Buying/renting prepackaged entertainment
Entering sweepstakes
Recreational vehicles
Patriotic activities and events

SUMMARY

Personal/Societal Affinities

Personal contentment/happiness with one's self—average
Belief in treating others fairly/ethically—above average
Affinity with local area/community—high
Affinity with country—high
Affinity with the global community—low

A Brief Psychological/Motivational Profile

Mainstayers are solid and stable people with firm convictions. They consider themselves strong, mainstream Americans and support American workers and American products. They are conventional people and believe strongly in following their country's traditions, laws, and mores. Their aim is to belong and to fit in. Their preference is for the known and the predictable. They try to live according to a strict personal spiritual or moral code and frequently are devout members of mainstream religions.

Religious and Spiritual Differences From the "Average" Portrait

Alone among the eight types, the majority of mainstayers do not believe that every religion is equally valid in the eyes of God and that someone can be a good person without believing in God; many consider themselves born-again Christians (along with temperates).

Some Words and Phrases to Help in Visualizing Mainstayers

Quiet evenings at home, fitting in, doing what is right, playing by the rules, watching television, patriotic, maintain a strong military, like parades, support economic protectionism, community events, resistant to change, volunteer fire department, Boy Scouts and Girl Scouts, criminals get too much coddling, flag burners should go to jail, hard to convince, see America first, buy American, brand loyal, do not much trust government or big business, about as likely to be male or female.

Personal Traits Frequently Respected by Others

Strongly value the concept of rule and consider it highly important to follow/play by the rules.

Personal Traits Not Universally Loved by Others

Can be intolerant of people with differing belief systems.

PORTRAIT OF A MAINSTAYER

Rose's face never reveals the struggles she is going through. She is one of those people whose inner peace shines through their faces. You knew at first glance that you would like Rose when you got to know her. Rose has gone through more misery and more trials and tribulations than her fair share, but in her heart of hearts she does not feel that way because she trusts in her Lord, and she knows that He never burdens His people with more than they can bear. And in the service of her Lord, she is going to handle the life she was dealt with grace and strength.

She is 37 years old, a widow, and has a 15-year-old daughter living at home. They live in the Black section of Paducah, Kentucky, and Rose has to work hard to earn a steady income in order to afford the house and provide for her daughter. She is currently working in a convalescent home on the other side of town that caters to elderly upper-middle-class

White people, many of whom are bedridden and/or suffering from dementia. Rose is Black, as are many of the other nurse's aides working at the facility. The job doesn't pay much, but the truth is that Rose really enjoys her job. She likes taking care of people and making them happy, and she is very good at it. Although many of the patients have difficulty in remembering who people are, interacting with Rose is frequently the high point of their day. She is unfailingly friendly and upbeat and has a marvelous way of talking with them about their infirmities in a jocular and comforting way that soothes all the patients and amuses those who are still sharp enough to understand the humor and good vibes in Rose's conversation.

Rose's life has not always been so tenuous financially. She had married early to a young Black college graduate who was on track for a successful career with one of the local factories, where he had risen to become a foreman. He enjoyed productive and positive relationships with the people he supervised, some of whom were Black and some of whom were White. Ken was well respected by the people he supervised and the people he reported to, both as a talented professional and as a good people person. He had a genuineness and a pleasant way of approaching and dealing with people that everyone appreciated.

His workers particularly liked the way he tried to make their jobs more successful and more pleasant. He would often stick his neck out to make sure that they always had the tools and supplies they needed to do their jobs properly. As in many factories, tools and supplies, being cost items, are resupplied only when they are totally worn out and have outlived their usefulness. What this translates into is workers being unable to maintain the desired levels of output quantity and quality, as the tools and supplies age and become less effective. This results in frustration among workers whose work ethic is high and an apathetic attitude among those who have concluded that there is little reason to respect the motivations and behaviors of their management. It was an unspoken law that foremen would hold off in issuing tools and supplies until the very end of their life in order to keep costs down.

Ken was very aware of the effects that working with inefficient tools had on his workers and would routinely extend himself in fighting with his management to see that his people had what they needed to do their jobs efficiently and happily. This was particularly crucial to the workers since theirs was an assembly-line operation. The speed of the line means that each worker had to do his or her job smoothly, quickly, and efficiently. These necessities were frequently jeopardized if the required tools and supplies were not up to par.

Up until the tragic accident, Rose and Ken and their two children enjoyed an almost idyllic family life. They owned a modest home in an up-and-coming neighborhood and their children were doing well at school and were well liked by their schoolmates and Sunday school-mates. All were active in their Baptist church community, and they had a wide circle of good friends. Life was treating them well and they were quite happy.

That was up to the untimely death of their 19-year-old, only son Matthew. He had finished 2 years at a prestigious midwestern engineering school on a football scholarship, a steady girlfriend, and a bright future. Like his father, he was charismatic, and people expected that he would also become a highly successful member of his community. He was killed in a freak accident during summer employment at a local factory when a steel beam being moved by a large crane inexplicably struck and crushed him.

The family was devastated. Although Rose was able to find a good measure of solace in her spiritual life, Ken was not so fortunate. His hopes and dreams were largely focused on his son, and with Matthew's death, he began to languish. His energy, vigor, and charisma began to fade, and although he tried his best to be stalwart at home and at work, his heart was not in it. Two years to the day from his son's death, he suffered a massive heart attack and died while at work. His friends said that he did not so much die from a heart attack as from a broken heart.

At that point, Rose's life changed forever. Ken had been the bread-winner, and she had been a dedicated and happy at-home mom. Her 15-year-old daughter Angelica was devastated as well, unfortunately carrying some of the guilt as the sole surviving child. She no longer had her earlier buoyancy and self-confidence, and she frequently felt at loose ends.

Faced with all this adversity, Rose proved to be more than resilient. What carried and sustained her was her unshakable conviction that "the good Lord never gives you more of a burden than you can manage." She was determined to create a positive home environment for Angelica and herself. Without Ken's income, however, they no longer could afford the home they had lived in for so many years, and Rose sold it. The proceeds were enough to enable them to buy a much more modest house in the predominantly Black section of town. Many of their church friends also lived in the neighborhood, and Rose and Angelica were rich in the company and comfort of their friends.

Although she did not consider herself a very "political" person, as she was exploring the various sources of aid for persons of limited income, she became aware that there was considerable pressure to eliminate various governmental programs that helped provide a "safety net" for people like herself. And she could not understand how people would allow that to happen, since the need for such programs was so apparent to her. Although she did not tend to ascribe labels to herself, if she had thought about it, she would have considered herself a staunchly liberal Democrat.

With only a partial pension from her husband's company, Rose had to find employment to carry herself and Angelica. Rose had graduated from high school but did not have any formal training for any particular profession or trade. But she had always loved helping people, and it was not long before she found employment as a nurse's aide at a local convalescent home catering to elderly, upper-middle-class White people.

5

Temperates

What Makes a Temperate?

CULTURAL CONNECTEDNESS

Following mainstayers, temperates are the next closest embodiment of American societal connectedness, support, adherence, and stability. They represent approximately 11% of the U.S. adult populace.

Like mainstayers, they too are strong supporters of American ideas, interests, policies, actions, economy, and products. They too feel a sense of close connectedness with their local communities, but not at as high a level as the mainstayers.

The principal ways in which they differ from mainstayers are the following: They are more amenable to change; are less resistant to ideas and influences from other countries; and are more open to the idea that America could, at times, be behaving less than perfectly appropriately within the world community. Even so, they are the strongest of all the eight types in support of the American economy and products.

They tend to be relatively uninterested in situations, events, and problems that occur outside of their own national borders. Their focus is primarily on things of concern within their own country.

Temperates are not much interested in exploring options beyond the local. They are happy and content with their ties and relationships to their local community and area. They prefer familiar destinations and locations for their pleasure trips and vacations.

They have little interest in traveling abroad or living abroad, even for a short time. Temperates believe that their own country has more sources of personal interest and pleasure than anyone could want and probably more than could be experienced in their lifetime. They want to get to know it thoroughly before they would consider visiting other countries. They do not expect that there would be much that would be of value or interest to them from other countries/cultures.

VALUES, ATTITUDES, AND MOTIVATIONAL MAKEUP

The philosophy of temperates centers on nonmaterialistic values and simple pleasures. They believe that money, possessions, and position are not indicators of real success in life. They reject extravagance as a concept, and many have chosen voluntary simplicity in their lifestyles. They are frugal and tend to have a strong outdoors orientation.

Above all, temperates are thrifty people. They are not impulsive buyers or spenders and will not pay exorbitantly to get what they want and need.

They are firm believers in the concept of voluntary simplicity. They reject the notions that money and happiness are equivalent and that success in life can be measured by money and possessions. Their focus is on being content and living simply. They are not at all focused on self-gratification, self-indulgence, or luxury for luxury's sake.

They are strong believers in living life according to high standards of spirituality, morality, and ethics. They are staunch practitioners of the Golden Rule in their personal dealings.

Overall, temperates are very happy with their status quo. They enjoy what they do. They are not avid readers and prefer watching television. They strongly prefer things that they know to things that are new to them. Similarly, they like their lives to be regular and predictable. They are happy with their established routines and are not easily bored by them. Temperates are predisposed to favor brands of products that they are familiar with. They tend to be loyal to them for long periods of time.

Temperates consider themselves conventional people and are happiest associating with similar people and taking part in conventional activities. They like to blend into their surroundings and do not like to be singled out for attention. They do not intentionally do things that will draw attention to themselves. They believe in working at what they like to do, being patient in the pursuit of vocational and financial goals, maintaining a focus on morals, and above all playing by the rules.

Temperates are not strongly competitive people by nature and are just as happy if they do not progress to positions of formal and recognized leadership.

They are conventional people with only average tolerance for change. They are the strongest of all the eight types in living according to high religious/spiritual/moral standards.

In comparison to the other types, they are average in the stability of their values and beliefs.

They do not believe in special advantage or privilege, either for themselves or for others. They believe in the correctness and appropriateness of equal levels of consideration and privilege for all. They believe strongly in the concept of following their culture's prevailing laws, rules, and mores. They do not believe that it is either right or appropriate for a person to take advantage of another, no matter what the circumstances.

They try to live according to their own strong sense of spirituality and morality.

They tend to be content with their status quo and do not feel compelled to expand their horizons, either intellectually or behaviorally. Their vocational emphasis is on doing well what they enjoy doing.

They have strong, conservative religious beliefs and are strongly committed to living according to these precepts. If they are associated with a formal religion (and they are likely to be), they tend to believe that that religion is uniquely "true." They tend to be not very tolerant of other religions, spiritual belief structures different from their own, or people who are outside of the cultural mainstream.

They do not favor equal roles and responsibilities for men and for women and are not supporters of feminist groups. They do not favor legitimizing rights and privileges for same-sex couples that would put them on an equal footing with heterosexual couples.

They are cautious, modest, unassuming, and conservative people who prefer to play it safe. They do not care for activities or pursuits that involve substantial elements of risk and/or danger. They do not much like to gamble or take part in games of chance.

They feel that life treats them fairly and feel strongly that they are successfully coping with life.

DEMOGRAPHIC TENDENCIES

There is substantial representation of temperates within all demographic categories and subgroups.

ACTIVITIES AND LIFESTYLES

Temperates' favored interests and activities focus on the themes of family and home. Their avocations suggest inexpensive sources of personal amusement and entertainment in keeping with their overall philosophy of frugality and voluntary simplification. They tend toward the peaceful and the serene and tend to stay away from activities that are oriented toward risk, danger, excitement, or thrills.

Their favorite activities and interests include the following:

Gardening
Walking for health
Home furnishing, decorating
Jogging, running, fast walking
Freshwater fishing
Raising houseplants
Crafts
Dieting, weight control
Self-improvement
Performing in a band/orchestra
Avid book reading
Time with grandchildren
Needlework/knitting
Sewing
Wildlife conservation
Collectibles/collections
Hiking/backpacking
Bible/devotional reading
Playing a musical instrument
Patriotic activities/events

SUMMARY

Personal/Societal Affinities

Personal contentment/happiness with one's self—average
Belief in treating others fairly/ethically—high
Affinity with local area/community—above average
Affinity with country—high
Affinity with the global community—below average

A Brief Psychological/Motivational Profile

Temperates hold strong nonmaterialistic values. They are frugal people and believe that money, possessions, and positions are not indicators of real success in life. They are content with who they are and what they are. They exemplify the concept of "voluntary simplicity." They are highly disposed to follow their country's laws, customs, and mores. They reject extravagance. They are strong supporters of the American culture, workers, and products. They tend to live according to their own strong sense of spirituality and morality. Their vocational emphasis is on doing something well that they enjoy doing.

Religious and Spiritual Differences From the "Average" Portrait

Many, along with mainstayers, consider themselves to be born-again Christians.

Some Words and Phrases to Help in Visualizing Temperates

Nonmaterialistic, frugal, focus on simplification, the job as more important than the money, reject extravagance, not impulsive, success in life and possessions are not the same thing, content with status quo, simple pleasures, temperate, judicious, like to watch television, not avid readers, support America, buy American, like the outdoors, never spend more than you must, treat people fairly, never take unfair advantage, don't buy just for the sake of buying.

Personal Traits Frequently Respected by Others

Try to be staunch practitioners of the Golden Rule in their everyday dealings with others.

Personal Traits Not Universally Loved by Others

Can be intolerant of people with differing belief systems.

PORTRAIT OF A TEMPERATE

Jim is now 65 years old and is thinking back on his life and how fortunate he has been and how he has turned out to be so successful while sticking to the rules and not having done anything major that he needed to be embarrassed about or afraid to have to defend in the afterlife.

He was a high school graduate from a small West Virginia town. His parents would have described themselves as middle-class or lower-middle-class people. His parents were devoted to each other and to their children, of which he was the oldest of three. The family was not the type that sent their children to college. What they aspired to was a steady job with a good, local company with which you might be fortunate enough to spend your entire working life. Because Jim had gotten good grades and shown a high aptitude in the mechanical drawing class, the family had dipped into its savings to send Jim to a trade school for a year to learn more about mechanical drawing.

When he had finished the course, he looked into the local paper's classifieds for job possibilities. Fortuitously, there was a help-wanted ad for a draftsman trainee at a small, local company that manufactured perfume. The job was in reference to helping design and set up a manufacturing process for a new company product that involved raw materials flow, coordination of numerous mixing and refining processes, and so on. Serendipitously, Jim's trade school final drafting class project had dealt with just those types of problems. Although Jim was not typically very outgoing or glib, on this particular day, he presented himself to the lead draftsman and the personnel manager very well and got the job. He was delighted at his good fortune. His starting salary was modest but still relatively close to what his father was accustomed to earning in the coal mines after 30 years on the job.

Before long, he found himself an important member of the drafting and engineering team and impressed his coworkers with his team spirit, his willingness to work, and his eagerness to make contributions to the project. In particular, the team leaders appreciated his willingness to do what he was told, to do it well, and to do it on time. From time to time, he thought of ways to improve upon what had been suggested and was able to bring these ideas to the attention of the team without seeming pushy or self-seeking. Jim was perfectly happy not to get major credit for these ideas, and when someone else was rewarded for breakthroughs that had been his ideas, it did not bother him very much. When the team leaders realized this self-effacing tendency, they appreciated him all the more, and he found that he was getting salary increases more rapidly than most and was beginning to reap the benefits of the esteem of his fellows. He was a happy camper.

It did not hurt anything that the new product utilizing these ideas and processes turned out to be a real money-maker for the company. They had gotten the jump on their competitors and had developed what proved to the best product in the category. Jim's contributions to this success did not go unnoticed by the company. His personnel file was full of laudatory commentary, and he caught the eye of top management because his work had contributed substantially to the success and the profitability of the new product and the company. After a time, he realized that he had become the principal technical person on the new process. And although he did not have any people reporting to him, he found that his status in the company was rising steadily, along with his income and prestige. Tragically, a year or two after the introduction of the new product, the senior draftsman was killed in a car accident, and Jim was made the senior draftsman for the company.

As the demand for the product grew, Jim was called upon to plan and oversee the construction of new facilities in other company locations to increase the production of the product. Before long, he had several draftsmen reporting to him, and although he did not revel in supervising these people, he did it well. He treated his people well; was fair with them; and since he demanded as much of himself as he did of them, he earned their trust and respect.

Being thrifty by nature, he saved much of the money he earned and invested much of it in company stock, which, because of his value to the company, he had an opportunity to buy on a very favorable basis.

Throughout this period, he had occasional casual dates, but he tended to be a loner and had remained single, dedicated primarily to doing his job and sending money back home to his family.

He attended most of the company's functions and parties, and it was there that he first noticed the striking, dark-haired, dark-eyed girl who had just joined the company. Marcia was 5 years his junior; was vivacious and pretty; and according to office scuttlebutt, was bound for good things within the company. Being somewhat reserved and having been rather unsuccessful with girls, Jim did not make a move on her. He soon found out, however, that she had been asking her friends about him, and he began to work his courage up to introduce himself to her. And as so often happens in these circumstances, she saved him the trouble. She contrived to hand-deliver a message from one of the company officers to him—which could just as easily have been handled through intracompany communications—and in the process, introduced herself to him. She engineered several more of these "chance" encounters, and Jim began to believe that she might like him.

Within the year, they were married. Marcia did more for Jim than anyone could possibly have imagined. She gave him all the love and affection he had been missing and the confidence that comes from knowing that you are highly valued and loved by someone you value and love. Before long, they had children—two sons and a daughter. They purchased a modest home a few miles from the company. Jim's life had never been better. He had been a family man in waiting, and he did not have to wait any longer. Marcia also filled in the spirituality that had been missing in Jim's life. His family had been desultory dropout Protestants. Marcia's family was avid in its Catholicism. And Marcia's two sisters were nuns, and she might have become one, too, but was too attracted by the secular opportunities that come easily to a person of beauty, personality, and intelligence. The possible differences in their spiritual philosophies disappeared as if by magic when Jim took the vows of the Church. And he hadn't taken them lightly. He was as good a member of the Church as a parish priest could desire.

Before long, he found himself a member of the church's Cub Scout Pack Committee, and after a few years, when his oldest son was of an age to join the pack, he became the cubmaster. He was an excellent cubmaster; not only did he believe firmly in the values that scouting taught, but he had an affinity for helping, teaching, and being with the boys. Although he probably wouldn't have admitted it, he also liked wearing the cubmaster uniform. Although he didn't gravitate to the spotlight or like to be conspicuous, he also took secret delight in being the visible leader of the cubs when they marched in the Fourth of July parade each year. He had to be careful during the patriotic ceremonies, however, as he was prone to sentimentality. and the singing of "The Star-Spangled Banner" would always bring him close to tears.

He had always thought of himself as patriotic and that he should contribute to the country's well-being. As a means of doing his duty to his country, he enlisted in a nearby army reserve unit. Part of his motivation had been to inject some excitement into his life, but he was not too surprised when the unit discovered his drafting/engineering expertise and slotted him into an opening they had in that specialty. Off he went to basic training and an additional course in the maintenance and construction of liquid transfer processes. He was back on his regular job within 4 months, with more valuable experience to the company than when he had left.

Meanwhile, the little fragrance company that Jim worked for underwent some startling changes. Due in part to the success of the product that Jim had been involved with, as well as derivative products that followed, the company grew to become one of the most prominent players in its industry, and the people who had been closely associated with its success, including Jim, were rewarded accordingly. After 20-some years with the company, he found that his bonuses and reinvested stock opportunities had grown to such an extent that he was no longer a man of merely modest means.

He noticed all this with some amazement and amusement. He had not had these objectives in mind at the beginning. What he had tried to do was to play by the rules, do his job well, not step on anybody's toes in his rise within the company, and in general be a good person. His overall reaction to his success, if he thought about it at all, was gratitude to the company for having hired him and given all the opportunities that had turned out so well, gratitude to his God and His Church, gratitude and thankfulness to his wife and family, and gratitude to his country for providing him the freedom to have achieved his potential to such an extent.

Although he was not argumentative about it, in his heart of hearts, he had little tolerance for people who did not share these sentiments, who were whiners, who did not "play by the rules," who behaved as though they were better than others, who did not support their country or its institutions, and who had no church connection.

But his good fortune had still not ended. Unexpectedly, the company's product line had become the focus of acquisition by two multinationals, who saw the company's capabilities as vastly increasing its possibilities in the world market. A bidding war developed in regard to a takeover of Jim's company, and when the dust had settled, Jim's personal net worth had grown into seven figures.

6

Doers

What Makes a Doer?

CULTURAL CONNECTEDNESS

Doers are the third closest type to the embodiment of the American cultural center. They represent approximately 12% of the U.S. adult populace. Doers are also supporters of America and American things and believers in adhering to its laws, codes, and mores, but not at the same level as mainstayers and temperates.

In comparison with all the other types, they are average in the strength of their levels of American beliefs and values, sense of community connectedness, and the importance they attach to living their lives according to high religious/spiritual/moral standards. They are also average in their level of conventionalism and in the stability of their values and beliefs.

Doers are not very open to foreign ideas and influences, nor do they have much tolerance for change.

They believe that it is important for their country to have a strong and capable military, even in times of peace, and believe that military service should be a required experience for the country's young men.

VALUES, ATTITUDES, AND MOTIVATIONAL MAKEUP

Doers are people whose focus, talents, and preoccupations are in the hands-on doing of things. Their orientation is toward the pragmatic accomplishment of specific tasks. Either by vocation or by temperament, they are people who like to build or fix things. They enjoy and are good at working with their hands and with tools. They enjoy owning and learning to use a variety of tools and love having the appropriate tool for a specific task. They are in their element when something in the household breaks down and they get to deal with it.

They are down-to-earth, sensible, and practical people who prefer to spend their time working with their hands rather than in theoretical or esoteric, intellectual pursuits. As truly hands-on people, they do not object to getting their hands dirty or to exposing themselves to less-than-clean conditions. They are not squeamish people.

Doers strongly prefer being outdoors to being indoors and tend to feel confined if they have to spend too much time indoors. Doers enjoy testing and challenging themselves against nature and its elements. They tend toward all outdoor activities, including such things as fishing, hunting, hiking, backpacking, and so on. Doers have a strong affinity for motorized vehicles and firearms and weapons of all types.

Doers are not materialistic. They favor simplicity and are not extravagant in their spending. Doers do not believe that wealth and possessions are indicators of a successful life.

They do not place great importance on formal religion and tend to have a "live and let live" philosophy about moral/spiritual belief systems and living in accordance with them. They are not strong believers in the concept of one "true" religion.

Doers do not favor the equalization of opportunity and responsibility for men and women. Neither do they favor legitimizing rights and privileges for same-sex couples.

Doers are always interested in something new. They have an expansive outlook and tend to get bored if they are forced to concentrate on only one thing or just a few things. They tend to prefer the new to things and circumstances they are already familiar with. They welcome the infusion of the new to break usual routines and patterns.

They are experimenters and like to try new and different things and activities. They are willing to forego what they know and like for the possibility of experiencing something new that they may come to know and like. Doers love excitement; they are active and vibrant people, always looking for activities and events that offer the prospect of excitement and thrills. They like to live on the edge. They like outdoor activities that most other people would not attempt—especially those that conspicuously call attention to the risk or danger or the skill involved in execution. They like games of chance. They like to gamble.

Doers prefer new destinations and locations for their vacations and pleasure trips.

Doers do not trust the motivations and behaviors of businesses and business leaders. They feel that they are not really concerned about the economic interests of the average person.

Doers feel the need for better/more effective protections for the national culture and its citizenry, especially in regard to a strong military; protections against foreign ideas and influences; protectionist policies that reference other countries' potential economic threat and dominance; containments against the power of big business; more effective legal, judicial, and law enforcement tools to combat criminals; eliminating corruption between politicians and special interests; making government more responsive to the needs of the average person, and so on.

DEMOGRAPHIC TENDENCIES

There is substantial representation of doers within all demographic categories and subgroups.

ACTIVITIES AND LIFESTYLES

Doers' levels of interests and activities are about half as extensive as those of explorers, but the intensity with which they pursue these interests is every bit the equal of explorers. The key themes of their favored pursuits are the physically active nature of the activities, taking place outdoors, the use of tools, involvement with off-road vehicles of all types, and involvement with weapons of all types.

The activities they favor are as follows:

Home workshop/do it yourself
Camping trips
Gardening
Watching sports on television
Buying/renting prepackaged entertainment
Hunting
Saltwater fishing
Raising houseplants
Swimming
Wildlife conservation
Doing automotive work
Time with grandchildren
Playing golf
Hiking/backpacking
Playing racquetball
Playing softball/baseball
Driving all-terrain vehicles
Bowling
Target/skeet/trap shooting
Health, natural foods
Fine art/antiques
Recreational vehicles
Playing volleyball
Playing a musical instrument
Environmental issues
Auto racing
Playing football
Power boating
Playing basketball
Science, new technologies
Off-road and street motorcycling
Water skiing
Investing in stocks, bonds
Playing tennis
Snow skiing, cross-country
Archery
Electronics
Snowmobiling

Performing in a band, orchestra
Skin/scuba diving
Flying aircraft
Ice-skating
Playing soccer
Sail boating
Hang gliding
Performing in a theater group
Playing softball/baseball

SUMMARY

Personal/Societal Affinities

Personal contentment/happiness with one's self—average
Believe in treating others fairly/ethically—average
Affinity with local area/community—average
Affinity with country—above average
Affinity with the global community—below average

A Brief Psychological/Motivational Profile

Doers are down-to-earth, sensible, and practical people whose principal focus, talents, and preoccupations are in the hands-on doing of things. Their orientation is toward the pragmatic accomplishment of specific tasks. Either by vocation or by temperament, they are people who like to build or fix things. They are skilled with manipulating and interacting with all sorts of tools, machinery, and equipment. They have a very strong predisposition toward spending time outdoors. They believe in following their country's laws and mores.

Religious and Spiritual Differences From the "Average" Portrait

Doers are less inclined to agree that living in accordance with their religious/spiritual beliefs is very important to them and that their moral standards are higher than most other people's.

Some Words and Phrases to Help in Visualizing Doers

Like tools, like working with their hands, do-it-yourselfers, like to build and repair, competitive, like roughing it, extreme conditions, like mechanical things, like taking things apart, like planning projects, not squeamish, like hardware stores, can never have too many tools, don't mind getting dirty, like motorized vehicles of all types, like weapons, four times as likely to be male as female.

Personal Traits Frequently Respected by Others

Are highly valued as friends and neighbors because of their practical talents and their love of being able to do things that others find helpful.

Personal Traits Not Universally Loved by Others

Can be somewhat rigid and nonpolitically correct in their beliefs concerning the appropriate societal roles for women.

PORTRAIT OF A DOER

Neighbors who knew him well thought that they could hardly have a better neighbor than Max. If you were asked to compile a composite of an ideal neighbor, you would come very close to describing Max. Max was a typical, middle-class, hard-working member of his community. At one time, he had had his own, relatively small construction company and was well regarded in the trade to be a versatile worker of many talents. All his life, he had been very capable in working with his hands.

In high school, when people were being divided into curricula according to their anticipated future vocations, Max had absolutely no trouble in deciding to specialize in shop courses as opposed to college prep or commercial classes. His father was a self-employed plumber, his mother a homemaker, and no one in his family had ever gone to college. Preliminary courses designed for college prep did not interest him, and he did not think he would do particularly well at them. Commercial courses seemed designed for girls and appeared too dainty for him. Shop courses—carpentry, metalworking, electricity, plumbing, and other hand-skills courses—seemed right up his alley. He thrived in them all.

When graduation approached, he thought that he might go into the military—he had always been a staunch supporter of his nation's armed forces. He especially yearned to learn to fly, and since there was still a cadet flight-training program open to high school graduates, he applied. However, he was disappointed when he was not accepted because of a deficiency in his night-vision capabilities.

Because of his father's connections in the local trades, he was soon accepted as an apprentice to a local contractor and before long became an up-and-coming jack-of-all-trades for the company. There was not a construction task that he could not master once he had tried it. But he was not well suited to the up and down nature of the construction business, and before long he quit and became a local law enforcement officer, primarily because of a larger, steady salary and union protection. By this time, he was married and had a baby boy. In his youth, he was most successful with women who were more submissive than aggressive, who deferred to him most of the time, and who fulfilled a chauvinist's expectations concerning women's role and happily (or at least contentedly) doing women's traditional chores.

Max's job was satisfying to him in a lot of ways. He liked the authority and the chain of command, and he liked being in charge of convicted lawbreakers. Off-hours he pursued all those adventurous, outdoor activities he had always loved—hunting, fishing, shooting, skiing, and hiking—and continued to buy, own, and fix up the many types of motor vehicles that had always been his passion—old cars of all types, ATVs, OHVs, snowmobiles, and the like.

To say he was a tool collector is a vast understatement. He was known by name to all the salesmen in all the local hardware stores; to frequent every flea market, garage, and estate sales; and to buy virtually every used tool for which he didn't have a duplicate—even those the purpose of which he wasn't exactly sure. This led him to buy every old cooking implement that came into his view, which in turn led him to try old cookbooks. This further led him to cook new dishes that made use of the tools. Over time, he became known as a gourmet cook, especially of dishes whose ingredients included game he had shot or fish he had caught.

Max was best known, however, as a good neighbor, one who would gladly—some would say eagerly—help you with any difficult home maintenance task you had.

Max's future ambition is to become—upon the chief's retirement—the chief of police of the small rural town where his family maintains a summer cabin.

7

Aspirers

What Makes an Aspirer?

CULTURAL CONNECTEDNESS

Aspirers rank fourth among the eight types in the closeness with which they represent the embodiment of American values and beliefs. They represent about 12% of the U.S. adult populace.

Compared to the other types, they are average in nationalistic beliefs/values, their support of America and things American, their sense of connectedness to their local communities, the degree to which they are resistant to influence/ideas from other countries/cultures, the stability of their values and beliefs, and their resistance to change.

However, they believe that it is important for their country to have a strong and capable military, even in times of peace. They lean toward the belief that military service should be mandatory for the country's young men.

Their most outstanding connections to the cultural center are their conventionalism—on which they rank by far the highest of all the types—and adherence to laws, rules, and regulations. They are also above average in the importance they attach to living according to high religious/spiritual/moral standards.

Aspirers tend to be moral and patient people who try to live according to the cultural rules. They consider themselves conventional and, in general, profess to believe in the rule of law.

They favor conventional spiritual/religious experience and tend to be not very tolerant of religions or belief structures different from their own or of people who are outside of the cultural mainstream.

VALUES, ATTITUDES, AND MOTIVATIONAL MAKEUP

Aspirers' main focus is in measuring up to those criteria that they consider reflective of society's highest standards. They hold themselves to high personal standards, including morals and physical condition. Their goals are status, personal recognition, making a good appearance, and making a good impression. They are competitive and have strong leadership aspirations.

They have little tolerance for the ordinary and the mundane and do everything possible so that others will not perceive them in those terms. They are highly competitive and seek to distinguish themselves from others by virtue of signs and symbols of superiority and exemplariness, including their physical condition, their dress, their possessions, and the attainment of high and recognized status.

Aspirers have a strong and positive sense of themselves. They have a strong ego and self-image. They consider that their moral standards exceed those of other people and that they are of higher status than most other people. In general, they tend to consider themselves as superior to others or on track to attain superior status. They believe that their accomplishments entitle them to special consideration and better treatment than other people.

Vocationally, they tend to gravitate to jobs that please them and also focus on high income. Aspirers do not look upon learning as a fun experience. They pursue education as a means to an end, not as an end in itself.

Aspirers do not easily change their minds. Once they have made a decision or judgment, they tend to stick with it.

Aspirers are predisposed to favor and to select familiar brand names. Their focus is on high prestige brands. They tend to be loyal to their favorite brands for long periods of time.

Aspirers are not homebodies. They prefer parties to quiet evenings at home. They seek stimulation of all types and are likely to drink alcoholic beverages.

Aspirers like excitement and are always on the lookout for activities and events that provide excitement and thrills. They like doing and trying new things and tend to seek out activities that promise elements of risk or danger. They like to gamble. For their vacations and pleasure trips, they prefer to go to places they have never been before.

They do not believe in equal roles or equal opportunity and responsibility for men and women. Nor are they enthusiasts for legitimizing rights and privileges for couples of the same sex.

DEMOGRAPHIC TENDENCIES

There is substantial representation of aspirers within all demographic categories and subgroups.

ACTIVITIES AND LIFESTYLES

The favored interests and activities of aspirers reflect their concern with status and their aspirations to being the best and appearing as the best to others—that is, measuring up to the highest standards.

This is reflected in their interest in Bible reading (absorbing the highest spiritual and moral teachings), aerobics and dieting/weight control (being fit and looking good), fashion/clothing (appearing their best), and home furnishing/decorating (presenting their home in the best possible light).

Some of aspirers' favorite activities and interests include the following:

Physical fitness/exercise
Watching sports on television
Jogging/running/fast walking
Buying/renting prepackaged entertainment
Self-improvement
Camping trips
Home furnishing/decorating
Fashion/clothing
Avid book reading
Weightlifting
Raising houseplants
Swimming
Bicycling
Time with grandchildren
Traveling outside the United States
Playing a musical instrument
Bowling

Health, natural foods
Bible/devotional reading
Attending cultural events
Driving ATVs
Fine art/antiques
Entering sweepstakes
Recreational vehicles
Playing volleyball
Hiking/backpacking
Environmental issues
Horseback riding
Investing in stocks/bonds
Power boating
Playing basketball
Target/skeet/trap shooting
Science fiction
Casino gambling
Off-road and street motorcycling
Playing tennis
Snow skiing, cross-country
Electronics
Real estate investment
Science/new technologies
Patriotic activities/events
Skin/scuba diving
Sail boating
Playing soccer
Flying aircraft
Performing in a band/orchestra
Archery
Studying/collecting wines
Performing in a theater group
Playing softball/baseball

SUMMARY

Personal/Societal Affinities

Personal contentment/happiness with one's self—average
Believe in treating others fairly/ethically—below average

Affinity with local area/community—average
Affinity with country—average
Affinity with the global community—average

A Brief Psychological/Motivational Profile

The main drive of the aspirers is in striving toward and measuring up to those criteria that they consider to represent the highest in personal standards. Their principal goals include personal success, personal recognition, achieving high status, making a good appearance, and making a good impression. They are highly competitive and seek to distinguish themselves from others by virtue of superiority in morals, personal standards, physical condition, dress, and the quantity and quality of their possessions. They are predisposed to behave in a highly conventional manner and to follow society's prevailing laws and mores.

Religious and Spiritual Differences From the "Average" Portrait

Aspirers are more likely to agree that someone can be a good person without believing in God, in some ways the Eastern religions are more appealing than Christianity, their moral standards are higher than most other people's.

Some Words and Phrases to Help in Visualizing Aspirers

Focus on achievement, high standards, only the best, right to the top, measure up, stay in shape, dress well, self-improvement, appearances are important, make a good impression, status counts, look important, status symbols, clothes make the man/woman, set themselves apart, competitive, energetic, self-satisfied, associate with/emulate important people, be the best you can be, avoid/do not associate with ordinary things/people.

Personal Traits Frequently Respected by Others

Hold themselves to high personal standards.

Personal Traits Not Universally Loved by Others

Can behave as if they were superior to other people/entitled to greater consideration and status.

PORTRAIT OF AN ASPIRER

Military service really suited Dawn, and she wasn't at all sure that she wanted to leave it. She had had a promising career as navy fighter pilot, and she had just finished her mandatory term of military service. She had an incredible resume, having graduated from the U.S. Naval Academy with a major in the sciences; completed flight school; been selected for the Navy's most advanced and sought-after fighter aircraft; and completed fighter pilot school, weapons training, and carrier duty. She was savvy enough to know that part of her success in having climbed the early steps up the ladder of success in naval aviation was due to a new atmosphere of increasing favorability in the armed services for women and her race (she is Black) and the fact that her father had also been a high-ranking navy pilot. She also had done very well academically in high school, was the vice president of the student body, was an outstanding soccer player, and was attractive enough to consider modeling as a career.

She recognized that staying in the military for her was dependent on the fact that changing international circumstances had prompted the national administration to consider cuts in the military budgets. She also realized that despite the fact that she had been on a fast track in the military, her future career progress in the navy was becoming more and more problematic in peacetime, where gender and race-related considerations were still in evidence. In addition, military pilots were being sought after and recruited more heavily by civilian corporations, especially by airlines and high-tech companies, which were going after people well trained in and familiar with the most modern technologies.

So at her age (late 20s), she knew she was a very desirable job candidate and figured the world was her oyster. She reasoned she had better take full advantage of her opportunities while she could. The outcome was that she had sent applications to many of the airlines for pilot positions and to several of the top-ranked graduate schools offering advanced technical programs in computers and avionics.

8

Empathizers

What Makes an Empathizer?

CULTURAL CONNECTEDNESS

Empathizers are the first of the types whose level of connectedness to core American beliefs, values, and motivations differ enough from mainstream thought to identify them as a divergent type rather than one of the congruent types. They represent about 10% of the U.S. adult populace.

Their principal distinguishing features are their high level of empathy toward and susceptibility to influences and ideas from other countries/cultures and their below average level of support for nationalistic beliefs and values.

On all other criteria, they tend to be about average in comparison to the other types: support for America and things American, adherence to its laws rules and regulations, a sense of connectedness to their local communities, their conventionalism, the importance they attach to living according to high religious/spiritual/moral standards, the stability of their values and beliefs, and their resistance to change.

Empathizers are not passionate supporters of their country and its actions within the world community. They tend to have a tolerant attitude toward people who are critical of this country and its actions. They believe that protection of free speech rights is vital, including those times when someone is vigorously expressing disapproval of this country's actions or behaviors.

Empathizers do not support the idea that their country requires a strong military force and feel even more keenly about this issue in reference to times of peace. They believe that military service should be strictly voluntary.

VALUES, ATTITUDES, AND MOTIVATIONAL MAKEUP

Empathizers have a broad field of vision and a universal perspective. They are perceptive of and responsive to the needs of others, irrespective of who they are or where they are located. Their perspective encompasses the world and all its peoples and species. As opposed to the four congruent groups previously described, their concerns stretch beyond national interests. Empathizers are "issuists," and the issues that concern them the most tend to be global and universal. They are concerned, for example, with the world's ecology, civil rights for all peoples in all countries, prevention of species extinction, overpopulation, and so on. In comparison to the congruent types, they do not have a strong allegiance to national boundaries or national interests. They feel that being guided solely by nationalistic concepts and interests can be and frequently is counterproductive to solving the world's problems, which they believe should take precedence over national interests, And they believe that America should act in a more responsive and responsible fashion toward achieving these goals.

When decisions are necessary that differentiate their country's national interests from the world communities', they will tend to be on the world's side of those decisions more so than any of the other types.

Empathizers believe that the benefits of the world's resources are disproportionately held by the major nations and that they should be shared more equally for the good of all peoples. They believe that everyone needs to face up to what they feel is the necessity of the world's wealth and resources being shared more fairly and equitably. Their concerns extend to animals as well as to people—they believe that there should be greater emphasis on protecting the rights of other animals/species.

Empathizers are deeply suspicious of the behaviors and the motivations of big business and the leaders of such business enterprises. They believe keenly that the interests of these institutions and leaders are at odds with the interests of people at large and the greater good that empathizers envision.

Empathizers don't trust government, the political process, or politicians. They are disappointed with their performance and leadership and do not believe that they are appropriately focused on the "universal good," fair play, and the world's citizenry.

Empathizers do not trust government and big business power centers to be very interested or very helpful in this process. They have concluded that everyone is going to have to make sacrifices for these global issues to be successfully addressed and do not trust business or government to either share these beliefs or willingly participate in the necessary processes.

In terms of their religious/spiritual beliefs, empathizers tend not to place great importance on formal religion. They tend to have a "live and let live" philosophy about spiritual/moral precepts and the necessity of living in strict accordance with them. They do not believe in the concept of one "true" religion.

Empathizers reject materialism as a personal philosophy. They are not focused on self-gratification, self-indulgence, or luxury. They tend not to be extravagant in their spending. They favor simplicity. They do not believe that the accumulation of money and possessions are indicators of having achieved success in life.

In general, empathizers are temperate, nonmaterialistic people who value simplicity and simple pleasures and try to live life according to a personally defined, appropriate spiritual and moral ethic.

Empathizers are very tolerant of religions or belief structures that are different from their own and/or are outside of the cultural mainstream. Similarly, they are very tolerant of people outside of the cultural mainstream.

They believe that it is inappropriate to seek special consideration and exemption from the rules that apply to society in general and do not believe that it is right or appropriate to take advantage of others under any circumstances.

Empathizers favor equal opportunity and responsibility for men and women and are champions for the idea of neutralizing the role differences between men and women. They also favor equalizing rights and privileges for couples of the same sex in comparison to heterosexual couples.

Empathizers tend to be home centered and stimulation avoiders. They tend to prefer quiet, home occasions to parties and to drink little alcohol.

For all the sensitivity they express toward others, however, Empathizers do not necessarily feel that life is treating them well or that they are successfully coping with life.

DEMOGRAPHIC TENDENCIES

There is substantial representation of empathizers within all demographic categories and subgroups.

ACTIVITIES AND LIFESTYLES

Empathizers tend to favor indoor, intellectual, and cultural pursuits, many of which do not involve physical activity. Their interests cover an eclectic range, suggesting an active mind interested in broadening its understanding: traveling, avid book reading, photography, environmental issues, gourmet cooking, and attending cultural/arts events. Their level of enthusiasm tends to be moderate. Some of their interests include the following:

Traveling in the United States and abroad
Walking for health
Avid book reading
Home furnishing/decorating
Physical fitness/exercise
Buying/renting prepackaged entertainment
Dieting/weight control
Raising houseplants
Fashion/clothing
Bible/devotional reading
Photography
Aerobics
Entering sweepstakes
Time with grandchildren
Environmental issues
Collectibles/collections
Saltwater fishing

Health/natural foods
Hiking/backpacking
Gourmet cooking
Doing automotive work
Investing in stocks/bonds
Attending cultural art events
Casino gambling

SUMMARY

Personal/Societal Affinities

Personal contentment/happiness with one's self—below average
Belief in treating others fairly/ethically—average
Affinity with local area/community—average
Affinity with country—below average
Affinity with the global community—very high

A Brief Psychological/Motivational Profile

Empathizers have a broad perspective and field of vision. They are attuned and sensitive to the needs and concerns of others, irrespective of where they are or what country they live in. They do not have a strong sense of nationalism and tend to believe that nationalism stands in the way of humankind's highest aspirations, potential, and achievements. They are distrustful of the motives of political and economic leaders and skeptical of their motives toward and connectedness with the "universal good," fair play, and the needs and rights of society at large. Their sensitivities and concerns extend to animals as well as to people.

Religious and Spiritual Differences From the "Average" Portrait

No meaningful differences.

Some Words and Phrases to Help in Visualizing Empathizers

Think globally, act locally; speak up; personal sacrifice for the universal good; save our planet; animal rights; nationalism does not work; challenge authority; environmental issues; share the earth's resources more equitably; good of all humankind; skepticism of governmental leaders; skepticism of big business, equally likely to be male or female.

Personal Traits Frequently Respected by Others

Have a highly sensitive and concerned perspective that encompasses all peoples and species.

Personal Traits Not Universally Loved by Others

When their country's national interests conflict with the world community's interests, they may well tend toward the world's side of those arguments.

PORTRAIT OF AN EMPATHIZER

Peter is now in his mid-50s. He teaches social sciences at a major university and travels extensively internationally, both as a visiting professor and for recreation. Although he certainly is intelligent enough to be the head of his department, he is not, probably because by nature he is not terribly competitive. He does not really care whether he leads or follows.

Peter was not always in academia. Earlier in life he was devoutly Catholic—first as an altar boy and later in his early manhood living in a monastery. He had always considered that he was well on track to becoming a priest. At about this time in his life, the Church underwent major upheaval, and Peter became disillusioned with the failure of the church to evolve into a more progressive, liberal, and universally focused institution. This was in conflict with his own personal philosophy, and he subsequently opted out of a formal vocational tie to the Church before ordination. Vocationally, he floundered for a period and held jobs connected with welfare, political activism, social work, and fund-raising for various charities. Eventually he settled—essentially by default—into teaching at the university level.

Peter has a tremendous natural gift for languages, and this proclivity, along with his great curiosity, has led him to a continuing interest in worldwide events. He speaks and can converse readily in more than a dozen languages, a talent that continues to grow as his travels take him to different countries and cultures. He converses easily with virtually all people he encounters and is well liked throughout a broad circle of friends.

With his gifts, Peter has been approached by political groups to participate in their agendas, but after brief flirtations with different party organizations, he has become increasingly skeptical and apathetic toward government and political groups, none of which, he feels, are oriented toward the good of all humankind. Consequently, philosophically and politically, he is content to sit quietly off to the side, reading voluminously and wondering if governments will ever come to their collective senses.

In sum, Peter has a highly sensitive and concerned perspective that encompasses all people. His perspective covers not only all peoples but also virtually all animal species. (He and his wife's principal avocation is heading up the local chapter of a national dog-rescue organization.) And over time, he has evolved into a vegetarian, at first because of his study of the relationship between eating animal flesh and human disease and gradually because of suspicions that there is much more spirituality in animals paralleling our own that we have yet to discover.

9

Enthusiasts

What Makes an Enthusiast?

CULTURAL CONNECTEDNESS

Enthusiasts—the second of the divergent types—ranks sixth out of the eight types in embodying core American beliefs, values, and motivations. They compose approximately 11% of the U.S. adult population. They are the first of the types to depart in dramatic ways from the cultural center.

Enthusiasts are average in their support for America and things American, their sense of connectedness to their local communities, their resistance to influences and ideas from other countries/cultures, and the stability of their values and beliefs.

They tend to be nationalistic. They support their country and its interests on many levels. They believe in protecting their country from attempts at influence from abroad. They support the country's economic system, its foreign policies, its products, and its ideas and philosophies. They tend to favor the notion that their country's interests take precedence over the interests of the world community.

Enthusiasts support their country and tend to think unfavorably of people who do not, be they citizens or foreign residents. They believe that residency and/or citizenship in this country should be reserved for people who truly and clearly value that opportunity. They believe that free speech that is directed toward criticism of the country can be carried too far.

Enthusiasts are below average in several important ways: their belief in the importance of adhering to society's laws, rules, and mores; their conventionalism; and their resistance to change.

They do not consider themselves mainstream—they are more inclined to think of themselves as out of the mainstream.

VALUES, ATTITUDES, AND MOTIVATIONAL MAKEUP

The principal motivations of enthusiasts relate to getting those material things and having those experiences that they believe make life worthwhile. They pursue what they consider to be life's pleasures and rewards, and their principal goals have to do with self-gratification, self-indulgence, and luxury.

They like money and enjoy the spending of money in order to get and have the best of what they want and can afford. They are materialistic. They believe that the appropriate accumulation of money and possessions are reflective of "success" in life.

Enthusiasts tend to be extravagant. They have a strong tolerance for spending what is required to get the things they want to have and to do.

They do not place great importance on formal religion. They tend to have a "live and let live" philosophy about living in accordance with moral/spiritual precepts and do not believe in the concept of one "true" religion. They are attracted to nonmainstream religions and tend to be tolerant of the belief structures and of people outside of the cultural mainstream.

They do not attach much personal relevance to the concept of obeying established rules. They tend to be willing to break or bend the rules to get what they want.

They are focused on their own interests and believe that on the playing field of life, it is perfectly appropriate to seek to take advantage of others, irrespective of society's view of the morals of such behaviors.

They view themselves as "privileged"—entitled to special consideration and exemption from those strictures that the culture has designed to apply to everyone. And in general, they tend to be less mindful of the culture's prevailing spiritual and moral ethic in achieving/getting what they want.

Enthusiasts do not care very much exactly what it is that they do to earn a living. They tend to be impatient in their pursuit of monetary goals and are among those most willing to shade moral and legal considerations to achieve their personal and financial goals.

They like to live on the edge. They like activities with strong elements of risk or danger that most other people would shy away from. They like games of chance. They like to gamble.

Enthusiasts have a strong need to be noticed. They like the limelight. They like to entertain and to be noticed. They will make themselves known. They prefer parties to quiet evenings at home. They like stimulation and are likely to enjoy alcoholic beverages.

They love excitement. They are active people, always looking for activities and events that offer the prospect of new thrills. They look upon learning as a recreational activity and like to continuously learn about new and different things, even if they can see no immediate use for them. For their vacations and pleasure trips, they prefer new destinations.

Enthusiasts are not among those who have strong mistrust of the behaviors and motivations of big business, government, the political process, or politicians in regard to protecting the economic interests and general well-being of the average person.

Enthusiasts like to purchase goods from direct outlets. Along with explorers, they are among those most likely to purchase things directly from catalogs, television infomercials, and websites. They are predisposed to favor and purchase familiar brand names. They tend to be loyal to such brands for long periods of time.

Enthusiasts rank among those least likely to have a positive self-image. However, they are not much interested in self-improvement. They are the type most likely to feel that they are having difficulty coping with life and that life is not treating them fairly.

DEMOGRAPHIC TENDENCIES

There is substantial representation of enthusiasts within all demographic categories and subgroups.

ACTIVITIES AND LIFESTYLES

The number of interests and activities that enthusiasts pursue is about two-thirds that of explorers. Theirs is an eclectic collection of interests, ranging from those both outdoors and indoors, physically active or passive, intellectual or not, and prestigious or more commonplace. One of the things that many of their favored avocations have in common is that they require heavy initial or continuing funding to pursue.

Some of enthusiasts' favored interests and activities include the following:

Buying/renting prepackaged entertainment
Watching sports on television
Physical fitness/exercise
Dieting/weight control
Fashion/clothing
Playing softball/baseball
Swimming
Gourmet cooking
Driving all-terrain vehicles
Aerobics
Traveling outside the United States
Snow skiing, downhill
Playing tennis
Doing automotive work
Bowling
Weightlifting
Casino gambling
Playing basketball
Saltwater fishing
Sewing
Playing volleyball
Health/natural foods
Entering sweepstakes
Recreational vehicles
Collectibles/collections
Power boating
Playing golf
Hiking/backpacking
Horseback riding
Electronics
Snow skiing, cross-country
Target/skeet/trap shooting

Doing needlework/knitting
Attending cultural art events
Playing football
Coin/stamp collecting
Off-road and street motorcycling
Water skiing
Investing in stocks/bonds
Playing racquetball
Snowmobiling
Ice-skating
Skin/scuba diving
Studying our nation's heritage
Auto racing
Patriotic activities/events
Science/new technologies
Real estate investment
Playing soccer
Archery
Studying/collecting wines
Sail boating
Flying aircraft
Performing in a band/orchestra
Hang gliding
Performing in a theater group

SUMMARY

Personal/Societal Affinities

Personal contentment/happiness with one's self—low
Belief in treating others fairly/ethically—very low
Affinity with local area/community—low
Affinity with country—below average
Affinity with the global community—average

A Brief Psychological/Motivational Profile

Enthusiasts are oriented toward the getting and the doing of the things that they believe make life worthwhile. They enjoy material possessions and pursue what they consider to be life's pleasures. They like money and enjoy the spending of money in order to get and to have the best of what it is they want. They tend to be impatient with things that stand in the way of these goals and will bend rules and regulations that they find inconvenient. Their principal focus and motivation is toward self-gratification.

Religious and Spiritual Differences From the "Average" Portrait

Enthusiasts are more likely to agree that someone can be a good person without believing in God.

Some Words and Phrases to Help in Visualizing Enthusiasts

Focus on getting and having what they want; materialistic; impulsive; extravagant; pay what it takes to get what they want; if you've got it, flaunt it; pleasure focused; acquisitive; luxuries make life worthwhile; equally likely to be male or female.

Personal Traits Frequently Respected by Others

Love excitement and can be extravagant in the entertaining and pleasing of others.

Personal Traits Not Universally Loved by Others

May behave as though it were appropriate to take unfair advantage of others.

PORTRAIT OF AN ENTHUSIAST

Marjorie thought that she had finally found her métier. She was making tons of money, she was doing something she enjoyed, and she was able to buy many of the things she had been used to having in life but that had been denied to her by recent circumstances.

And truthfully, having money was very important to her. She didn't really care precisely where her money came from or what she did for a living, as long as it was very lucrative.

Although she glorified the status and prestige of her current job in talking to others about it, the truth of the matter was that she was a telemarketer and spent the bulk of her day on the phone trying to convince people to do things that she wanted them to do. She was essentially a salesperson.

The two main motivators for her doing this job were to provide for her children and to return to a secure and prosperous financial situation. She was a single mom. She and her husband had recently divorced. George had been a brilliant and creative wunderkind of an electronic engineer and had been associated with one of Silicon Valley's most glamorous start-ups when they met. She had been young, not yet out of college, and she had been swept off her feet by this low-key, handsome success of a man who suddenly came into her life. She was convinced that this was the man she wanted to spend the rest of her life with, and he felt similarly.

She had been an only child of comfortably fixed parents who had indulged her. In particular, she was the apple of her father's eye, and he was hard-pressed to deny her anything. Consequently, she had grown up accustomed to getting the finest of just about every material thing she had wanted, when she wanted it. If she knew the definition of the words "thrift," "budget," and "deferred gratification," there was no evidence of it either in her life with her parents or in her marriage. She and George had become accustomed to spending the household's considerable income as though there were no tomorrow.

In the early heyday of their marriage, this had been no problem. The same type of indulgence that had been lavished upon her by her parents was similarly available to her with her new husband. Before long, they had two daughters, whom she indulged just as vigorously as she had been indulged growing up.

When Silicon Valley fell onto harder times, so did their marriage. Her husband's job disappeared. The company no longer was in an expansion mode, and the next-generation products he had been developing disappeared—as did the company itself several months later. And, of course, the stock options that had defined their anticipated future wealth had become worthless. Another casualty was George's self-esteem and self-confidence.

With the downturn in her husband's career, economic fortunes, and personality, strains came upon their marriage. She had also learned from one of her company friends that George had been having an affair with his secretary. The reality was that that was no longer an issue, since his secretary had also lost her job and no longer had any interest in George. This led to an increase in his drinking from the "heavy social" to the "heavy all the time" category, and he had a clear case of depression. Although they tried a trial separation to see if he could get his act together, that did not happen, and they subsequently divorced.

Marjorie obtained custody of the children, and she found that she needed to become the household's breadwinner. She was at some disadvantage in the down economy because she had not finished her college degree before marrying George. Although she had never held a full-time job of her own, she was determined to continue the household's lifestyle, even though she had never stopped to think what her working skills might be, how marketable they might be, and how successful she might prove to be as a breadwinner.

Although she felt somewhat insecure about her abilities, the truth was that she had a combination of talents and skills that ultimately proved to be very marketable. One of her considerable skills was that she was an excellent conversationalist—she had always done beautifully in the myriad of cocktail parties she had gone to with George, and she had a gift of gab that was matched only by the self-confidence with which she presented her opinions. She spoke loudly, quickly, and with seeming authority. Many people found it intimidating to engage in conversation with her because of these skills and characteristics. She would frequently prevail in argument merely through the sheer force of her presentation. Even so, she had not realized what a powerful asset this could be in the business world.

Because of her lack of a college degree, she knew that many career paths would not be open to her. Fortuitously, one of her friends told her that she was a natural for sales. This struck an immediate responsive chord with her, because she liked the idea of matching wits with someone to get him or her to do something she wanted them to do, especially when it was for her own personal benefit. After all, she had had great experience manipulating her father and her ex-husband, and this seemed right up her alley.

She had long thought that being an executive recruiter would be a wonderful occupation—on the one hand helping people to find more worthwhile employment and on the other hand in helping employers find better employees—all while being rewarded handsomely for doing so.

After a relatively short job search, she landed a job with a Silicon Valley recruiting firm. They had given her a short battery of aptitude tests, and she had scored close to their "ideal recruiter" profile. She was somewhat surprised to learn that executive recruiting was essentially a telemarketing job. But as it developed, she was beautifully suited for this profession. She was a charming person to talk to on the telephone, even if a shade pushy in advancing her agenda.

The realities of the job were nowhere near as glamorous or high status as she had imagined. Her job workplace was simply a large room—an open bullpen—with modest desks, telephones, and a personal computer for each of the recruiters. It took her a while to be able to disregard the telephone conversations that other recruiters were involved with all around her.

The first step in the recruiter's job was to locate an employer who was conducting or was about to conduct a search for a new employee. Each recruiter was assigned a "specialty" that was his/her exclusive domain with the firm. Hers was high-tech engineering people within the computer industry. This proved to be a natural fit for Marjorie because of her extensive familiarity with these types of people due to her ex-husband's involvement. It not only gave her a general first-hand understanding of what these people did and also some ability to speak their language. A secondary benefit was that it gave her several acquaintances with whom she could begin the cold-calling to locate the influentials who were responsible for the job assignments.

The telephone cold-calling process began with a call to the company switchboard—semiscripted screening to try to identify hiring influentials (not the personnel department staff, who were deemed to be competitors and not facilitators). It was in this process that persistence, charm, aggressiveness, seeming sincerity, and a certain sly deviousness were the key attributes to identifying and getting to talk to these people. Once she had identified and talked to the hiring authority, she had to try to convince him/her that he/she should entrust the assignment to her and her firm alone. Assignments undertaken on this exclusive basis offered a greater probability of success and would allow her to earn her commission. Recruiters did not earn any commission unless they actually produced the new employee that was hired by the client.

Once the job order had been obtained, then she had to identify appropriate prospects and convince them to let her present them to the hiring authority. This was a tricky proposition, because these cold-call telephone contacts were of necessity made during working hours, and most frequently the prospect did not know her. So she had to earn the trust of the prospect, establish the prospect's suitably for the client's position, and convince the prospect that this was something not only worthwhile but highly desirable for them to consider—all without revealing the hiring company to the prospect (or else the prospect might be tempted to go after the job without Marjorie's involvement). It took a certain type of person to do all this well, and Marjorie did it very well!

Recruiters quickly learned that there was very little in the way of social service aspects to their job. Very seldom were people who were currently unemployed found to be desirable by the hiring authority. The reasoning was that if they were truly capable, they would not be unemployed. So recruiters typically learned to maintain a certain psychological distance from the unemployed who would call the firm hoping that a recruiter could help them. The unspoken truth of the matter was that most hiring influentials were hoping that the recruiter knew of and could steal a talented employee from a major competitor who was doing the exact job description that they were trying to fill.

The job also required a certain ability to press desirable prospects to consider/take the new job without much consideration for, or evaluation of, the prospect's real needs, hopes, and ambitions. Although certain job opportunities would turn out to be wonderful for the prospect, that was not always the case. Sometimes, a recruiter would facilitate a change to a company less desirable than the one the prospect previously worked for, to a job with a less desirable career track, or to a boss less desirable than the one he/she had. Some jobs entailed moving to another area of the country, which might or might not be a desirable thing. Most recruiters considered all these possibilities to be a case of "caveat emptor" and didn't worry a lot about it. Consequently, recruiters tended to "oversell" the new opportunity—to gild the lily, as it were.

The principal thing was to get the commission, which could be, and frequently was, substantial. The actual commission structure in Marjorie's office was a sliding scale based on the total volume of commissions he/she had earned within a given period of time. So the prospect for substantial income was there, and Marjorie shortly became one of the top producers in her firm, earning a six-figure-plus income.

Although she was working long hours under heavy-handed management and pressure to produce and not seeing much of her daughters, she was making good money, she was able to provide for them in much the style of their predivorce household and to provide quality child care during her working hours, and she was able once again to indulge her own passions for fine material possessions and pricey off-the-job activities and avocations.

Marjory had found that these circumstances were very acceptable to her.

Nonconventionals

What Makes a Nonconventional?

TWO COUNTERCULTURAL TYPES

The final two divergent types—nonconventionals and explorers—can both essentially be considered countercultural. They differ in substantial ways from all other types described earlier but also differ in important ways from each other.

CULTURAL CONNECTEDNESS

Nonconventionals are the furthest distanced from the cultural center among all the eight types on virtually all the criteria described in previous chapters. They comprise approximately 11% of the U.S. adult populace. As their name would suggest, they are by far the most unconventional of all the types.

They rank last among all the types on the degree to which they hold nationalistic values and beliefs; their support for America and things American; their adherence to America's laws, regulations, and cultural mores; their sense of connectedness with their local communities; and the personal importance they attach to living according to high religious/spiritual/moral standards.

Nonconventionals do not have a strong nationalistic point of view about their country and its interests within the world community. They do not much believe that the country needs protection against the influences from other countries. They are not strongly supportive of the nation's military and do not support the idea of a strong military force, especially in times of peace. They believe that military service should be strictly on a voluntary basis.

They have no strong predilection to buy products/services produced in their own country versus similar products/services produced elsewhere in the world.

They are not strong supporters of their country and its actions. They have a very tolerant attitude toward people who are openly critical of their country. They are strong supporters of the right of free speech, even when someone flagrantly and ostentatiously disapproves of the country's behaviors, actions, or policies.

They are very open to influences and ideas from other countries and cultures. Like explorers and enthusiasts, they embrace change. And like explorers, their values and beliefs are highly unstable.

VALUES, ATTITUDES, AND MOTIVATIONAL MAKEUP

Nonconventionals consider themselves strongly unconventional and tend to operate outside of the established cultural, organizational, and legal guidelines that are characteristic of society's "mainstream."

Compared to the other types, they have little sympathy with the established order of things and have adopted different attitudes, beliefs, and behaviors. They tend to have a "live and let live" philosophy and tend to be tolerant, permissive, self-indulgent, broad-minded, and liberal. In their attitudes and behaviors, they can be counted on to be nonconformists, to do the unexpected, and to disregard the bounds of convention. They believe in the legalization of drugs for private use.

Their self-image includes lower moral standards than the norm, impatience, and a willingness to bend or break the rules as they see fit. Philosophically, they place little value on playing by the rules. They tend to be focused on their own interests and are not mindful of the culture's current spiritual and moral ethic in achieving what they want.

They also tend to be materialistic and believe that money and possessions are reflective of success in life. Vocationally, they are not terribly concerned with how they earn their living. They are more focused on the earning of money than on the nature of the task that they are doing. They are not particularly competitive and do not care whether they are in leadership positions.

Nonconventionals do not place great importance on the beliefs and practices of formal religion and do not subscribe to the concept of one "true" religion. They tend to be very tolerant of other people's belief systems and of people who—as they are themselves—are out of the cultural mainstream. If they are interested in religion at all, it is frequently an interest in nonmainstream religions or belief systems.

They are not particularly impressed with their formal schooling experiences. They feel that much of the things they are/were exposed to are not terribly valuable in real life.

They do not much care for manual labor or tasks that require the use of hand tools. They do not like getting their hands dirty and are not much interested in building or fixing things.

Nonconventionals prefer parties to quiet occasions at home and are likely to enjoy partaking of alcoholic beverages and other mood-altering substances.

Nonconventionals believe that males and females should be as equal in their opportunities and responsibilities as they wish to be. They also favor legitimizing equal rights and privileges for couples of the same sex.

Nonconventionals are generally unconcerned about threats or potential threats to their country or to its interests. They are content with the existing mechanisms of protection of the nation and its citizenry. They are essentially unworried about the adequacies of the military; foreign relations; the role of the country within the international community; the role of big business; the state of the legal, judicial, and law enforcement arms of the country; the containment of corruption between politicians and special interests; the degree of government responsiveness to the needs of the average person; and so on.

DEMOGRAPHIC TENDENCIES

There is substantial representation of nonconventionals within all demographic categories and subgroups.

ACTIVITIES AND LIFESTYLES

Nonconventionals have a limited number of interests and activities—about one-quarter that of explorers—and are considerably less avid with them as are explorers. The entertainment activities they most favor suggest a solitary, stay-at-home focus (as opposed to the group focus typical of many of the explorers' activities) and an emphasis on modes of favored transportation (motorcycling, all-terrain vehicles, horseback riding, etc.).

Some of the interests and activities typical of what nonconventionals favor include the following:

Buying/renting prepackaged entertainment
Avid book reading
Entering sweepstakes
Bowling
Driving all-terrain vehicles
Off-road and street motorcycling
Horseback riding
Power boating
Playing football
Auto racing
Snow skiing, cross-country
Target/skeet/trap shooting
Ice-skating
Snowmobiling

Conspicuous by their absence are activities focusing on self-improvements in fitness, health, and appearance.

SUMMARY

Personal/Societal Affinities

Personal contentment/happiness with one's self—below average
Believe in treating others fairly/ethically—low
Affinity with local area/community—below average

Affinity with country—low

Affinity with the global community—average

A Brief Psychological/Motivational Profile

Nonconventionals tend to operate outside of the established guidelines that are characteristic of society's "mainstream." They are impatient, offbeat, and will bend or break the rules if necessary to do or to get what they want. They have little sympathy with the established order of things. They tend to have a "live and let live" philosophy and tend to be tolerant, permissive, broad-minded, and self-indulgent. In their attitudes and behaviors, they are highly likely to be nonconformists, to do the unexpected, and to stretch the bounds of convention.

Religious and Spiritual Differences From "Average" Profile

Nonconventionals are less likely to agree that, as the Bible says, the world literally was created in 6 days. Living in accordance with their religious/spiritual beliefs is very unimportant to them. They are not at all likely to be born-again Christians. Their moral standards are lower than most other people's. They are more likely to agree that every religion is equally valid in the eyes of God and that someone can be a good person without believing in God.

Some Words and Phrases to Help in Visualizing Nonconventionals

Offbeat; unconventional; freethinkers; originals; breaking the mold; fad starters; spontaneous; nontraditional; countercultural; change for the sake of change; outrageous clothes/hairstyles/cosmetics; the totally new and different; don't expect the expected; the laws, rules, and regulations don't apply; what everyone else is willing to accept isn't very good; new religions; out-of-the-box thinking; equally likely to be male or female.

Personal Traits Frequently Respected by Others

Tend to be very tolerant of other people's belief systems and of people out of the mainstream.

Personal Traits Not Universally Loved by Others

May not "play by the rules" in achieving what they want.

PORTRAIT OF A NONCONVENTIONAL

Bill had always been somewhat of a loner, and his interests centered on the outdoors. He was not much of an athlete and did not have much in the way of physical grace. But he was energetic, was an avid hunter and fisherman, enjoyed hiking and camping, and generally was happy with just about every outdoor activity. In high school, he had been a "college prep" student, so when he graduated—having nothing more specific in mind—he thought that forestry would be as good a major as anything else.

Since he had earned better-than-average grades, he had no trouble being accepted into the forestry and wildlife management program at a major eastern college. Although he did not particularly care for many of the courses that were required for this major (chemistry, botany, and zoology, to name a few), he completed his courses with the required B level of performance and graduated with his degree in four years.

Following graduation, he found employment in the fisheries' management department with one of the eastern states bordering the Great Lakes. For those who knew him, this seemed to be an ideal job for him—but that did not prove to be the case. Although he did not anticipate it when he accepted the job, most of his time was not to be spent in the great outdoors but rather involved laboratory work designed to better understand the life patterns of several different kinds of fish. In the initial instance, he found himself assigned to the study of the lamprey—a predator, eellike creature that attached itself to and sucked the life out of lake trout and other large, commercially valuable sport fish in the Great Lakes system. Although he understood the benefits of eliminating the lamprey as a threat to sport fish, he took little satisfaction in the study of how that might be accomplished.

After a year on the job, he found that his boyhood enthusiasms for the outdoors and his perhaps overly romanticized anticipations concerning the nature of his job were not being satisfied. Summarily, he quit. As he was fond of telling his friends, except for the occasional opportunity to fish in desirable areas little known to others, "the rest of the job sucks."

His next career thought was that he wanted to make as much money as possible as quickly as possible, so that he would be able to devote the majority of his time to those outdoor recreational activities that he truly enjoyed. The best financial career path to accomplish this, he felt, would be to become a lawyer. And so, he applied to and was accepted by an eastern law school. He did well and received his law degree in 3 years. At this point, he decided he no longer cared for "the formality of the east," left his eastern roots behind him, and moved to California. He was pleased that he was able to intern with a California law firm known for its success in obtaining large personal injury settlements for its clients. His thought was that not only could he make a lot of money, he might also be doing good for deserving people who needed help, who had been wronged by "the system" and needed a good legal advocate. After a little over a year, he passed the California bar on his first attempt.

It was at this point that he was the most optimistic he had ever been, and he treated himself to a new Japanese SUV, in which he began to again pursue those wilderness activities that he dearly loved.

The job didn't turn out to be what he had expected. He had made this career choice believing that, in the cases he worked, he would essentially function as a well-armed David battling evil Goliaths for good, unfairly treated people who would be worthy of good representation. He felt that with his best efforts and talents, justice would prevail and that in the end, deserving clients would receive just treatment and be financially well rewarded. And in the process, because of the hefty contingency fees of the profession, he would similarly be well rewarded.

The reality was that, as the most junior legal staff member, he did not share substantially in the massive amounts of money in fees that the firm produced. As is true of many such firms, the most senior partners got the most prestigious and most lucrative assignments as well as the bulk of the monies that eventuated from their successful handling of these types of litigations. What Bill initially got to do was low-level filings and background research needed in the prosecution of these cases. And he learned that frequently, at the conclusion of the successful pursuit of these cases, many clients did not receive the settlements that Bill thought were fair and just.

But Bill's disillusionment was not all attached to the doings of his firm. After a number of cases had put him in closer contact with the client group, he found that many of them did not turn out to be the blameless saints that he had anticipated helping. In fact, some of them were outright frauds, hoping to cash in on some minor incident. He remembered an incident where a strapping physical specimen of a man who did heavy labor in a refuse disposal facility was suing the county government for total disability because he was no longer able to work at all. The man had slipped on a wet surface, had tumbled into a trash compactor pit, and barely avoided being crushed. What he did do, however, was to wrench his back severely and was no longer able to stretch, reach, or lift heavy items—or so his doctor testified—and that the injury had completely taken away the man's ability to earn a living as a laborer. Bill found himself very simpatico with this man and hoped he would get a substantial settlement from the county.

It looked like that would be the case until the insurance firm representing the county presented its final arguments. The critical evidence was a film prepared by a private investigator, who had been hired to follow the man. On the final day of surveillance, their persistence was rewarded. The investigator had followed the man to his brother's home, and he watched and photographed him happily building a stone wall fence—digging trenches; making cement; lifting, carrying, and placing large boulders; and so on. It also turned out that the physician who had testified to the man's disability seemed to have a specialty in this area. He had done the same thing for other people numerous times. He was generally suspected as being for hire in these matters, and he had also been charged with medical fraud several times, of which charges he had never been convicted.

Several such incidents had eroded much of Bill's faith in the goodness of his fellow man and their institutions and laws, and he found his interest in this type of law slipping fast. His decreased motivation was soon apparent to his firm's seniors, and before long, he was offered the opportunity to resign.

He next opened his own law firm, convinced to take only well-supported cases for the truly wronged. Unpopular cases and causes seemed to gravitate to him and he to them. If there were an unpopular person or a person of an unpopular type in society's eyes who was in trouble, they would appear on Bill's doorstep and become his clients. One of his most memorable cases was a suit on behalf of a transvestite who claimed that the city police had beaten him severely after he had been arrested on a drunk and disorderly charge. Although many people had been present at the alleged beating, none was willing to testify, and Bill did not have the financial resources to match the legal effort that the city could mount. Although the case got a lot of coverage in the media, it was yet another unsuccessful effort for Bill.

But he never turned such cases away. The more hopeless the prospects for the successful prosecution of the case, the more avidly Bill seemed to pursue them. This was not a formula for financial success in the legal profession, and it was not long before the disastrous economics of his practice caught up with him. During this period, he changed his address many times, sold his Japanese SUV, and bought a 5-year-old Harley-Davidson chopper.

Again, he found himself without a job or a career path that he wanted to pursue. And by this time, he had concluded that his idea of success in life was quite different from that of most other people. And he had pretty well concluded that the chances of his becoming a financial "success" were slim. This, he was surprised to conclude, didn't bother him, and he found that he was content to take jobs that allowed him to earn a survival or slightly better wage, as long as he didn't have to "put up with the bullshit" that conventional career paths entailed.

He currently is a relatively contented, if not happy man. He now lives in the foothills of a western state and is earning a survivable income as a part-time paralegal and as a part-time salesman for a large used car and truck lot.

Explorers

What Makes an Explorer?

CULTURAL CONNECTEDNESS

Explorers represent about 13% of the U.S. adult populace. They are above average in the degree to which they hold nationalistic beliefs and values but are below average on all other cultural connectedness criteria described in previous chapters.

Of all the types, they are the most open to influence/ideas from other countries/cultures; they are the second most unconventional; and they are the least likely to adhere to society's laws, rules, and cultural mores (tied with nonconventionals). They are below average on their support for America and things American; their sense of connectedness with their local community; and the degree to which they feel it is important to live according to high religious, spiritual, or moral standards. They embrace change. Of all the types, their values and belief systems are the most unstable (tied with nonconventionals).

They are totally receptive to options beyond the local. They do not feel strongly connected to their local community and area. They are quite receptive to the idea of foreign travel and living abroad for a time.

They do not have a strongly nationalistic point of view about their country and its role within the world community. They do not believe that their country needs protection from the influences from other countries. They have no strong preference for buying products/services produced in their country versus similar products/services produced elsewhere.

They do not support the idea of a strong military force, especially in times of peace. They believe that military service should be strictly voluntary.

They are not at all xenophobic. Although they support their country, they tend to have a "live and let live" attitude toward people who are critical of this country or its actions. They believe that the rights of free speech should be supported, even when someone is vigorously exhibiting disapproval or criticism of the country's actions.

They are culturally expansive. They have broad and encompassing cultural horizons. They think that it is a wide and wonderful world and want to experience as much of it as they can. They do not believe that their country is the be-all and end-all of all the good things in life. They are very interested in and open to ideas and influences from other countries and cultures.

VALUES, ATTITUDES, AND MOTIVATIONAL MAKEUP

Explorers are vibrant, active, and energetic people who like to live "on the edge." They are active both physically and intellectually. They can be counted on to be among the first to try or do something new. They enjoy being thought of as unconventional. They like to be on the forefront of everything, and they have a strong attraction for and curiosity about the new. They prefer the new to things they have already experienced. They tend to be easily bored. They like the infusion of the new to break usual or monotonous routine. They are always looking for new activities and new learnings. Routine bores them, and they engage in many activities just for change and variety's sake. They thrive on the unfamiliar, especially if it entails risk, excitement, and new thrills. They prefer new destinations for their vacations and pleasure trips.

They have a strong need to be noticed. They like the limelight. Explorers like parties. They prefer parties to quiet evenings at home and are likely to enjoy alcoholic beverages. They like to entertain others. Explorers do not sit quietly in the corner at parties. They will definitely make themselves known. Explorers are competitive and have strong leadership aspirations.

They seek out activities that most other people would not attempt, especially those that conspicuously call attention to their inherent risk or danger. They like games of chance. They like life's gambles. They love excitement. They are always looking for activities and events that offer the prospect of new thrills.

They have so many interests that others are likely to view them as unfocused and scattered. In a group setting, they tend to be talkative. Their high levels of energy and extroversion lead other people to think of them as "full of themselves."

They consider themselves unconventional. Many of their thought processes and behaviors fall outside of the usual cultural modes and strictures. They are not strong believers in playing according to the rules. They tend to be willing to break or bend the rules to get what they want. They believe that it is perfectly all right to take advantage of other people, irrespective of how society may view the "rightness" or "wrongness" of such behaviors.

Explorers are happy with themselves and have a strong and positive self-image. They tend to feel somewhat privileged and believe that they are entitled to special consideration and exemption from the rules that society expects everyone to follow.

Explorers do not place great importance on formal religion. They tend to have a "live and let live" philosophy about moral/spiritual precepts and living in strict accordance with them. They do not believe in the concept of one "true" religion. They tend to approve of legalizing drugs for personal use.

They have strong interest in experimentation. They like new and different things and activities. They are willing to forego what they know and like against the possibility of experiencing something new that they may come to know and like.

They are not overly concerned about being familiar with the brands of the products they buy. They tend to experiment among brands and do not develop the lasting attachments to individual brands that is characteristic of others of the types.

Explorers are academically oriented. They are happy with the time they have spent in school. They enjoy the academic environment and value the things that they learn/have learned in school. They look upon learning as a recreational activity. They like to continuously learn new and different things, even if they can see no immediate need or use for the information.

Explorers are open-minded about reconsidering past judgments and decisions. They will reevaluate circumstances based on new or additional information and act accordingly.

Explorers favor equal rights, opportunities, and responsibilities for men and women. They are opposed to the idea that women should stay within the traditional homemaking and caregiving model. They also favor legitimizing rights and privileges for same-sex couples.

They are not among those who are mistrustful of big business, government, the political process, or politicians in regard to looking out for the interests of the average person.

They are content with the existing mechanisms of protection of the national culture and its citizenry. They do not tend to be critical of the current state of the military; foreign relations; the role of the country within the international community; the role of big business; the adequacy of the legal, judicial, and law enforcement arms of the country; containment of corruption between politicians and special interests; the level of government concern and responsiveness to the needs of the average person; and so on.

DEMOGRAPHIC TENDENCIES

There is substantial representation of explorers within all demographic categories and subgroups.

ACTIVITIES AND LIFESTYLES

Explorers participate in more activities, hobbies, and avocations with more intensity than any of the other types. They are above average participants in 69 out of 81 activities measured, 8 times as many activities as the lowest-ranked types, and they participate with considerably more intensity than any of the other types.

Explorers favor active, vigorous, competitive outdoor sports, games, and activities of many types. They enhance their physical fitness by working out. Many of the activities they favor have a group rather than an individual focus.

Interestingly, one of explorers' major interests is studying our nation's heritage, even though they do not score highly in other ways on their connectedness to their country and their culture. We believe that this is related to the fact that being an explorer, for most, will be a transitional phase before they move on to becoming one of the other types.

Some of explorers' favored interests and activities include the following:

Traveling within the United States and abroad
Physical fitness/exercise
Home furnishing/decorating
Buying/renting prepackaged entertainment
Camping trips
Watching sports on television
Bicycling
Gardening
Swimming
Fashion/clothing
Jogging/running/fast walking
Raising houseplants
Crafts
Dieting/weight control
Freshwater fishing
Avid book reading
Snow skiing, downhill
Aerobics
Playing softball/baseball
Attending cultural/arts events
Weightlifting
Wildlife conservation
Environmental issues
Hiking/backpacking
Self-improvement
Playing volleyball
Playing golf
Photography
Gourmet cooking
Playing racquetball
Playing football
Playing basketball

Sewing
Science fiction
Playing tennis
Water skiing
Power boating
Fine art/antiques
Health/natural foods
Driving all-terrain vehicles
Saltwater fishing
Recreational vehicles
Collectibles/collections
Horseback riding
Playing a musical instrument
Bible/devotional reading
Skin/scuba diving
Doing needlework/knitting
Science/new technologies
Target/skeet/trap shooting
Casino gambling
Electronics
Playing soccer
Studying nation's heritage
Investing in stocks/bonds
Street motorcycling
Patriotic activities/events
Auto racing
Archery
Flying aircraft
Ice-skating
Studying/collecting wines
Performing in a theater group
Performing in a band/orchestra
Snowmobiling
Real estate investment
Hang gliding

SUMMARY

Personal/Societal Affinities

Personal contentment/happiness with one's self—average
Believe in treating others fairly/ethically—average
Affinity with local area/community—below average
Affinity with country—average
Affinity with the global community—average

A Brief Psychological/Motivational Profile

Explorers are active, energetic, and extroverted people who like to "push the envelope." They are always among the first to try new experiences, activities, and sports, especially physically demanding ones that offer the prospect of risk, excitement, and new thrills. They seek the limelight and love to entertain. They pursue the different and the untried, just for change and variety's sake. They are often trendsetters. They do not mind behaving unconventionally and have few qualms about bending or breaking the existing rules. They have strong interest in experiencing other countries and other cultures.

Religious and Spiritual Differences From "Average" Profile

Explorers are more likely to disagree that, as the Bible says, the world literally was created in 6 days. They are not born-again Christians. They are more likely to agree that someone can be a good person without believing in God. They find that in some ways, the eastern religions are more appealing than Christianity. They believe their moral standards are higher than most other people's.

Some Words and Phrases to Help in Visualizing Explorers

Extremely active and energetic; physical; adventuresome; experimental; talkative; love excitement, new thrills, to show off, to try something new, to go out, challenge, and risk; vital and vigorous; open-minded; bold; unafraid; exhibitionistic; willful; competitive.

Personal Traits Frequently Respected by Others

Explorers are people whose energies, enthusiasms, interests, ideas, and charisma can be appealing and contagious to others in their orbit.

Personal Traits Not Universally Loved by Others

They are frequently likely to behave outside of accepted cultural modes and strictures.

PORTRAIT OF AN EXPLORER

Bruce, at 46, has had a modestly successful career as a CPA, which bores him no end. He really doesn't identify with his age group, who he feels were too settled into repetitive and boring lifestyles. Life for him was pursuing the things he liked to do and forever was on the lookout for new challenges. When his 22-year-old son made his first parachute jump, he was tied up with a client meeting and couldn't go with him.

Otherwise, he surely would have, even though he was well aware of the possibilities of broken ankles and various other assaults to his anatomy. Although he had lost some of his earlier high-risk orientation, he still was not afraid to try things that stretched his physical abilities, which he reluctantly had to admit were not the equal of what they had been only a few years ago. In moments of candid introspection, he remembered that when he was younger, he had wanted to be a movie stuntman and that he had wisely concluded that he didn't really have the athletic abilities of the legendary Hollywood stuntmen. (One of his heroes was Yakima Canutt, the first stuntman to do the very dangerous stunt that involved leaping from the stagecoach driver's seat, climbing over all the galloping horses, dropping to the ground, letting the horses and stage pass over him, grabbing onto the rear of the stage, climbing up and over the stage, subduing the bad guy on top of the stage, gaining control of the reins, and bringing the stage to a safe stop.)

He realized that many of his adult friends considered him either immature or a case of arrested development, but he was who he was and he was happy with that. He also realized that he preferred the company of his son's friends to people his own age. To get to do the things he liked to do required younger, more adventuresome companions, and he found them much more lively and humorous than others of his own age.

He liked to fish, to play cards, to gamble, and to engage in activities that made people laugh. He'd do almost anything for a laugh. Although he couldn't remember ever having put a lampshade on his head at a party, doing something like that was not beyond him. Parties at his house were never quiet affairs. He was not embarrassed by boisterousness or by people who, like himself, would do almost anything for a laugh.

He was an accomplished instrumentalist and was a principal player in the local community bands and orchestras. He had a combo that played at wedding receptions and other social affairs and was also an actor in the local little theater group.

He loved words and wordplay and could never resist making a joke or a pun out of what someone else might have said. It was hard to get the last word in with him. Those who didn't like him sometimes found this exasperating. People whose conversation was mainly composed of facts and things factual tended to bore him, and he would typically disengage mentally from those kinds of conversations. In group conversations, he was sometimes quiet, usually because he didn't have an original thought in his mind to insert. (Originality was very important to him.) For these reasons, some people thought of him as off, some thought of him as amusing, some people thought of him as charismatic, and others thought of him as boring.

Currently, one of his real passions is fishing. However, he doesn't fish often. He just wants to fish "well," with a real opportunity to catch something "worthwhile." His long-term goal is to travel to places where trophy fish were likely to be, to fish with knowledgeable guides, and to catch (and release) a good example of the particular variety. Toward that end, he has fished for marlin off Mexico and Hawaii, for salmon in Alaska, for smallmouth bass in New Brunswick, and for brook trout in Labrador. One of his current hopes is to catch a rare California golden trout before they have become extinct.

Psychodynamic Types by Age

PSYCHODYNAMIC TYPE TENDENCIES BY AGE

The tendency to be one or another of the psychodynamic types varies substantially by age. Some of the types have their roots deep in values and beliefs developed before the age of 18. Other types take more time to develop and have their fruition at varying age levels. The tendency to be one or another of the psychodynamic types is clearly related to life stage and increasing life experience.

PSYCHODYNAMIC TYPES AMONG MINORS

Before the age of 18, people are exposed to life under the control of parents and other older adults. Their reflection of this existence can be expected to be influenced by the prevailing attitudes in the household and balanced between the objectives of the adults and their own desires. During this period, they are more likely to be divergents than congruents by a 63% to 37% margin. In the 10- to 14-year-old cohort, they are most likely to be enthusiasts (I want what I want when I want it), nonconventionals (I disagree with the prevailing rules and regulations), and aspirers (I want to be the leader). In the 15- to 17-year-old cohort, they are more likely to be nonconventionals (1 don't agree with much that is going on around here), aspirers (I'd like to lead), empathizers (I'm sure learning a lot about the world), and enthusiasts (I still want what I want when I want it).

The 18- to 24-year-old cohort is a watershed in terms of being one or another of the psychodynamic types. In the 18- to 24-year-old cohort, people begin to establish their own identities relatively free from the constraining influences of their previous living experience. At this point, we see a substantial drop in the mainstayer values (with its emphasis on the tried, the true, and the routine), a substantial rise in explorer values (as they spread their wings to try more of life's adventures), a rise in aspirer values (as they gear up to achieve their desired place of leadership and wealth in the world), a rise in enthusiast values (as they try to begin to satisfy their material wants and desires), and a drop in nonconventional values (as they realize that some degree of conventionality and compliance is valued in much of the world's endeavors). At this point, divergent types still outnumber congruent types 66% to 34%.

Beginning at the 25- to 29-age cohort, things really begin to change. There is a substantial decrease in the numbers of divergent types (53%) and a corresponding increase in the numbers of the congruent types (47%). There is an 9% increase in the mainstayer category, an 8% drop in the explorer category (as people cut down on their high risk and high energy focus), an 8% drop in the enthusiast category (as people gain some additional understanding of the acquisition and payment process), a 7% increase in the empathizer category (as people gain a better understanding of their place in a larger world), a 6% increase in the temperate category (as people realize that money is not the solution to all the world's problems), a 4% drop in the aspirer category (as people begin to discover that not everyone will become one of society's leaders), and a 4% drop in the nonconventional category (with increasing understanding that being different may not accommodate other of their goals).

Between 30 and 34, further changes occur, but not dramatically. Divergents still outnumber congruents by a 56% to 44% margin.

By the 35- to 39-age cohort, congruents have become the majority by a 54% to 46% margin over the divergents. Among the significant changes, mainstayers, temperates, and doers have gained ground, and aspirers, enthusiasts, nonconventionals, and explorers have all lost ground. Never in any of the ensuing age cohorts will divergent types outnumber congruent types.

From the 40- to 44-age cohort on, with an occasional blip, the following general trends occur: Mainstayers continue to grow in number and become predominant over the other types. At the end of the traditional working life—age 64—congruent types outnumber divergent types by a 66% to 34% margin.

In the early phase of retirement, beginning at age 65, there is a temporary surge in the explorer category (as newly available time allows for the revisiting of opportunities that people might like to pursue). At the same time, the tendency to be a temperate drops substantially (as people loosen frugal ways to more fully enjoy life).

At age 70, there is further change as the tendencies to be an explorer drop again, a temperate increase again, and a doer increase substantially (as people tend to turn more to activities associated with tools and handicrafts).

Psychodynamic Types—Percentage Distributions by Age Cohort—Percentages Read Across

	Congruent types					Divergent types		
	Main-stayers	Temperates	Doers	Aspirers	Empa-thizers	Enthusiasts	Noncon-ventionals	Explorers
Total U.S. adults	20	11	12	12	10	11	11	13
Individual age cohorts (projected distributions)								
10–14*	11	3	6	17	15	26	17	5
15–17*	11	4	8	14	14	13	26	10
18–24	3	2	9	20	5	18	18	25
25–29	12	8	11	16	12	10	14	17
30–34	10	13	8	13	10	14	15	17
35–39	15	16	14	9	10	12	12	12
40–44	19	10	8	16	14	9	11	13
45–49	21	16	15	10	9	9	12	8
50–54	20	13	15	8	18	13	4	9
55–59	42	11	21	5	5	7	2	7
60–64	27	16	13	10	13	5	13	3
65–69	38	5	12	6	13	5	10	11
70–74	42	11	27	5	3	7	5	**
75+	36	16	12	14	4	9	2	7

* = Percentages within these cohorts interpolated from a geographically balanced, 2,600-case survey independent of the 3,800-case benchmark survey data represented by the rest of the table.

** = Less than 1/2 of 1%.

Psychodynamic Types—Percentage Distributions by Age—Percentages Read Down

Age—U.S. adults	Congruent types				Divergent types			
	Main-stayers	Temperates	Doers	Aspirers	Empa-thizers	Enthusiasts	Noncon-ventionals	Explorers
18–24	2	2	10	22	6	23	22	27
25–29	7	9	11	15	16	11	15	15
30–34	6	15	8	12	12	15	16	17
35–39	8	15	11	8	11	11	11	10
40–44	10	10	7	13	15	8	10	10
45–49	8	10	9	6	6	6	8	5
50–54	6	7	7	4	11	7	2	4
55–59	12	6	10	2	3	3	1	3
60–64	8	9	6	5	8	3	7	1
65–69	11	3	6	3	8	3	5	5
70–74	9	4	9	2	1	3	2	*
75+	13	11	7	8	3	6	1	4

* = Less than 1/2 of 1%.

MAINSTAYERS

Mainstayers are by far the largest of the eight types, representing 20% of the U.S. adult populace. However, the tendency to be a mainstayer begins slowly and does not reach large numbers until adulthood. The tendency to be a mainstayer accelerates quickly after that. By 35–39, it has become the largest group. From there, it remains the largest of all types and increases its lead over all other types throughout all other age cohorts. The level of its representation remains relatively stable from 40 to 44 but accelerates its dominance rapidly after that until it peaks at 70–74 with 43% of that age cohort.

Mainstayers are the most stable of all groups. The data suggest that once people migrate from other types into the mainstayer type, they tend to stay mainstayers. (This conjecture is not provable from current data, however.)

TEMPERATES

Temperates are the smallest of the eight groups within the 18–24 age cohort, with only 2% of the total and an estimated 11% of the U.S. adult populace. By age 25–29, the tendency to have become a temperate has already been well established; by age 30–34, the tendency has taken firm hold, and the representation of this type remains relatively constant after that. The data suggest that there may be a surge in the tendency to be a temperate at 60–64. As noted, the representation of temperates among the age cohorts tends to be stable.

DOERS

Doers are the fifth largest group within the 18–24 age cohort, representing an estimated 12% of the U.S. adult populace. The tendency to be a doer is already fully established by 25–29, slowly and inconsistently advances until 45–49, and peaks at 70–74.

ASPIRERS

Aspirers are the second largest type in the 18–24 cohort, representing an estimated 12% of the U.S. adult populace. The predisposition to be an aspirer is fully established as early as age 10. It drops a bit after 24 and it peaks in the 40–44 age cohort and peaks again in the 75+ cohort.

EMPATHIZERS

Empathizers are the fifth largest type in the 18–24 cohort, representing an estimated 10% of the U.S. adult populace. The tendency to be an empathizer is fully established as early as age 10 and is relatively stable throughout ensuing age cohorts, with the exception of the 18–24 cohort. It peaks at 50–54 and remains strong up until 69.

ENTHUSIASTS

Enthusiasts are tied with nonconventionals as the third largest type in the 18–24 cohort, representing an estimated 11% of the U.S. adult populace. The tendency to be an enthusiast is fully established as early as age 10, drops off dramatically prior to adulthood, and then continues on a relatively stable basis with perhaps a slight decline in the later years.

NONCONVENTIONALS

Nonconventionals, representing 11% of the total U.S. adult populace, are tied for the third type within the 18–24 age cohort. The tendency to be an nonconventional is fully established by 18–24. However, they (and explorers) tend to be an unstable type, and their representation within ensuing age cohorts is inconsistent.

EXPLORERS

Explorers are the largest type within the 18–24 cohort, representing 25% of the total and an estimated 13% of the U.S. adult populace. The tendency to be an explorer is fully established by 18–24. However, as was the case with the nonconventionals, explorers are an unstable type, and their representation declines rather consistently throughout all ensuing age cohorts. The tendency to be an Explorer peaks in very early adulthood.

REPRESENTATION AMONG THE CONGRUENT TYPES COMPARED WITH THE DIVERGENT TYPES

Only within the cohorts up to 30–34 are the congruent types (mainstayers, temperates, doers, and aspirers) outnumbered by the divergent types (empathizers, enthusiasts, nonconventionals, and explorers). The margin in the 30–34 cohort is 47% versus 53%.

After that, congruents consistently and increasingly outnumber divergents, beginning at 55% versus 45% in the 35–39 cohort and increasing to 85% versus 15% in the 70–74 cohort.

13

Special Age Cohorts

The Myths of the Baby Boomers and Generation X

Marketers and advertisers, especially advertising agencies, are always looking for new ways to conceptualize people in order to more successfully penetrate the markets they are interested in. Two special-case cohorts that have gotten immense amounts of attention have been baby boomers and generation Xers.

Baby boomers are usually described as those people born during the years 1946–1964. The marketing theory is that, because of the unique circumstances of this time period, these people will share common and compelling characteristics and motivations and therefore can essentially be treated as a unified segment to be marketed to as though it were one target segment. In addition, baby boomers are typically believed to be a special case segment within the U.S. populace. As far-fetched as that might sound, this theory had, and still has, a surprising degree of acceptance.

However, this segment has substantial representation from each of the eight psychodynamics types, as follows. Obviously, the attitudes and motivations of the eight types have considerable variation.

Mainstayers—22%
Temperates—13%

Doers—13%
Aspirers—11%
Empathizers—12%
Enthusiasts—10%
Nonconventionals—9%
Explorers—10%

People within generation X are usually described as that segment of the population that was born between 1965 and 1976. As with the baby boomers, they are frequently advertised and marketed to as though they were an entity with consistent attitudes and motivations. This also is not true. It is true, however, that the pattern of distribution of the psychodynamic types is quite different from that of the baby boomers. The distribution of the psychodynamic types within the generation X age cohort is as follows:

Mainstayers—12%
Temperates—13%
Doers—11%
Aspirers—13%
Empathizers—10%
Enthusiasts—12%
Nonconventionals—14%
Explorers—15%

Psychodynamic Types—Percentage Distributions by Popular Age Cohort Descriptors

	Congruent types				Divergent types			
	Main-stayers	Temperates	Doers	Aspirers	Empa-thizers	Enthusiasts	Noncon-ventionals	Explorers
Total U.S. adults	20	11	12	12	10	11	11	13
Individual age cohorts (projected distributions)								
Preadulthood/adolescence*	11	4	7	17	15	15	23	8
Early adulthood	3	2	9	20	5	18	18	25
Generation X	12	13	11	13	10	12	14	15
Baby boomers	22	13	13	11	12	10	9	10
Preretirement	35	14	17	7	9	6	7	5
Retirement—first phase	40	8	19	6	8	6	8	6
Retirement—later phase	36	16	12	14	4	9	2	7

* = Percentages within this cohort interpolated from a geographically balanced, 2,676-case survey independent of the 3,800-case projectable benchmark survey data represented by the rest of the table.

14

Psychodynamic Types by Ethnicity

There are considerable differences in the distribution of the psychodynamic types according to ethnicity.

The distribution of psychodynamic types among Whites/Caucasians hews very closely to the overall pattern among the U.S. population as a whole, with 57% being congruent types and 43% from the divergent types. There is no more than a 1% to 2% variance by type compared with the population as a whole. There are almost twice as many Whites as any other type who are mainstayers, with approximately 20% of Whites comprising the mainstayer group.

For Blacks, congruents make up about 61% of the population and divergents only about 40%. Mainstayers and aspirers are about tied for being the most heavily represented of the eight types, at 24% and 23%, respectively.

Hispanics are considerably more heavily represented among the divergent types, with 60% represented among the four divergent types. Representation is fairly equally divided among the four divergent types, with 14% to 18% in each type.

Asians are even more heavily represented among the four divergent types, with 78% coming from these four types and only 22% representation from the four congruent types.

The remaining ethnic groups load heavily among the four divergent types, with 55% from those types and 45% from the four congruent types. Doers are the most significantly represented of the types among the "other" ethnicity groups.

Percentages of Psychodynamic Types Within Ethnic Groups—Percentages Read Across

	Congruent types				Divergent types			
	Main-stayers	Temperates	Doers	Aspirers	Empa-thizers	Enthusiasts	Noncon-ventionals	Explorers
Total U.S. adults	20	11	12	12	10	11	11	13
White	20	13	13	11	8	11	12	12
Black	24	7	7	23	15	8	7	10
Hispanic	6	6	14	13	14	13	15	18
Asian	3	1	12	6	13	21	9	35
Other ethnicity	3	8	29	5	13	8	13	21

Percentage Distributions of Psychodynamic Types by Ethnic Groupings—Percentages Read Down

	Congruent types				Divergent types			
	Main-stayers	Temperates	Doers	Aspirers	Empa-thizers	Enthusiasts	Noncon-ventionals	Explorers
White	82	87	79	68	64	75	78	70
Black	15	8	6	21	18	9	7	9
Hispanic	3	5	9	9	13	10	11	12
Asian	*	*	3	1	4	5	2	8
Other ethnicity	*	1	3	1	2	1	1	2

* = Less than 1/2 of 1%.

15

Psychodynamic Types by Geography

CENSUS DISTRICT AND REGION POPULATION DISTRIBUTIONS THROUGHOUT THE UNITED STATES

There are nine major census regions/districts, which are described in this chapter, as well as the percentage of the U.S. population residing in each region/district, based on recent census information:

Northeast—18.2%

New England—4.8%
>   Maine, Vermont, New Hampshire, Massachusetts, Rhode Island, Connecticut

Mid-Atlantic—13.5%
>   New York, Pennsylvania, New Jersey

Midwest—22.1%

East North Central—15.3%
>   Wisconsin, Michigan, Illinois, Indiana, Ohio

West North Central—6.8%
>   North Dakota, South Dakota, Nebraska, Kansas, Minnesota, Iowa, Missouri

South—34.9%

South Atlantic—17.3%
> Delaware; Maryland; Washington, DC; Virginia; West Virginia;
> North Carolina; South Carolina; Georgia; Florida

East South Central—6.7%
> Kentucky, Tennessee, Mississippi, Alabama

West South Central—12.0%
> Oklahoma, Arkansas, Texas, Louisiana

West—23.7%

Mountain—7.3%
> Montana, Idaho, Wyoming, Nevada, Utah, Colorado, Arizona,
> New Mexico

Pacific—16.4%
> Washington, Oregon, California, Alaska, Hawaii

Psychodynamics by Census Regions/Divisions

	Congruent types	Divergent types
Total U.S. adults	55%	45%
Northeast	44%	56%
New England	41%	59%
Mid-Atlantic	45%	55%
Midwest	64%	36%
East North Central	60%	40%
West North Central	71%	30%
South	60%	40%
South Atlantic	57%	43%
East South Central	83%	17%
West South Central	58%	42%
West	45%	56%
Mountain	45%	55%
Pacific	45%	56%

Psychodynamic Types by Census Regions/Divisions

	Congruent types					Divergent types		
	Main-stayers	Temperates	Doers	Aspirers	Empa-thizers	Enthusiasts	Noncon-ventionals	Explorers
Total U.S. adult	20%	11%	12%	12%	10%	11%	11%	13%
Northeast	10%	5%	18%	11%	8%	11%	20%	17%
New England	9%	1%	26%	5%	13%	10%	30%	6%
Mid-Atlantic	10%	7%	15%	13%	6%	12%	16%	21%
Midwest	30%	12%	11%	11%	8%	9%	11%	9%
East North central	21%	14%	14%	10%	7%	11%	13%	9%
West north central	46%	7%	6%	12%	10%	4%	7%	9%
South	22%	11%	14%	13%	9%	11%	8%	12%
South Atlantic	19%	11%	13%	14%	11%	15%	9%	8%
East south central	43%	14%	23%	3%	3%	2%	5%	7%
West south central	19%	11%	12%	16%	8%	9%	8%	17%
West	12%	10%	8%	15%	11%	14%	16%	15%
Mountain	13%	13%	7%	13%	5%	19%	11%	21%
Pacific	12%	9%	8%	16%	13%	12%	18%	13%

ANALYSIS

The data reaffirm much of the lore concerning where the values of the American public center. Keep in mind that the following table, reading the columns from left to right, shows the types with the strongest American values and beliefs on the left (congruent types) and the types with the weaker American values and beliefs on the right (divergent types). The table can be read progressively from left to right in this regard.

East South Central, East North Central, West South Central, West North Central, and South Atlantic are the regions where people with core American values and beliefs (congruent types) are more concentrated. Countercultural values and beliefs (divergent types) are more prevalent in the New England, Mid-Atlantic, Mountain, and Pacific regions.

STATES WITH HIGHER-THAN-AVERAGE CONCENTRATIONS OF THE TYPES

The following text shows which states have higher-than-average proportions of the eight psychodynamic types.

Mainstayers—national percentage = 20%

Missouri—68%
Alabama—68%
Kentucky—34%
Minnesota—33%
Tennessee—32%
Michigan—31%
North Carolina—30%
Indiana—29%
Ohio—28%
West Virginia—28%
Maryland—24%
Mississippi—23%
Texas—21%

Temperates—national percentage = 11%

Kentucky—29%
Indiana—27%
West Virginia—25%
Colorado—20%
North Carolina—19%
Illinois—16%
Mississippi—16%
New York—12%
Ohio—12%

Doers—national percentage = 12%

Tennessee—31%
Mississippi—29%
Kentucky—26%
Michigan—22%
Massachusetts—18%
South Carolina—17%
Arizona—17%
New York—17%
Colorado—17%
Indiana—17%
Florida—16%
Maryland—14%
Wisconsin—13%

Aspirers—national percentage = 12%

Washington, DC—85%
Virginia—42%
Arizona—24%
Pennsylvania—21%
Florida—18%
Texas—17%
Alaska—16%
Minnesota—15%

California—15%
Ohio—15%
Missouri—14%
Illinois—14%
Washington—13%

Empathizers—national percentage = 10%

South Carolina—24%
West Virginia—22%
Maryland—17%
Iowa—17%
California—16%
Wisconsin—13%
Minnesota—13%
Illinois—11%
Alaska—11%

Enthusiasts—national percentage = 11%

North Carolina—20%
South Carolina—20%
Louisiana—19%
New Jersey—18%
Pennsylvania—16%
Florida—16%
Washington—15%
West Virginia—13%
Wisconsin—12%

Nonconventionals—national percentage = 11%

Massachusetts—40%
Pennsylvania—37%
Washington—35%
Wisconsin—30%
Iowa—23%
Virginia—23%

Alaska—23%
Ohio—19%
New York—16%
California—13%
Louisiana—12%
Maryland—12%
North Carolina—12%

Explorers—national percentage = 13%

New Jersey—53%
Arizona—32%
Mississippi—23%
Louisiana—21%
South Carolina—20%
Texas—18%
Minnesota—18%
Colorado—16%
Illinois—15%
Washington—15%
California—14%

	Congruent types				Divergent types			
	Main-stayers	*Tem-perates*	*Doers*	*Aspirers*	*Empa-thizers*	*Enthu-siasts*	*Non-conven-tionals*	*Explor-ers*
States in the north-east census region	10%	5%	18%	11%	8%	11%	20%	17%

New England

Massachusetts has higher than national proportions of the following:
      Nonconventionals—40%
      Doers—18%

Mid-Atlantic

New York has higher than national proportions of the following:
    Nonconventionals—16%
    Doers—17%
    Temperates—12%
New Jersey has higher than national proportions of the following:
    Explorers—53%
    Enthusiasts—16%
Pennsylvania has higher than national proportions of the following:
    Nonconventionals—37%
    Aspirers—21%
    Enthusiasts—16%

	Congruent types				Divergent types			
	Main-stayers	Tem-perates	Doers	Aspirers	Empa-thizers	Enthu-siasts	Non-conven-tionals	Explor-ers
States in the mid-west census region	30%	12%	11%	11%	8%	9%	11%	9%

East North Central

Ohio has higher than national proportions of the following:
    Mainstayers—28%
    Nonconventionals—19%
    Aspirers—15%
Indiana has higher than national proportions of the following:
    Mainstayers—29%
    Temperates—27%
    Doers—17%
Illinois has higher than national proportions of the following:
    Temperates—16%
    Explorers—15%
    Aspirers—14%
    Empathizers—11%

Michigan has higher than national proportions of the following:
    Mainstayers—31%
    Doers—22%
    Enthusiasts—15%
Wisconsin has higher than national proportions of the following:
    Nonconventionals—30%
    Empathizers—13%
    Doers—13%
    Enthusiasts—12%

West North Central

Minnesota has higher than national proportions of the following:
    Mainstayers—33%
    Explorers—18%
    Aspirers—15%
    Empathizers—13%
Iowa has higher than national proportions of the following:
    Nonconventionals—23%
    Empathizers—17%
    Doers—14%
Missouri has higher than national proportions of the following:
    Mainstayers—68%
    Aspirers—14%

	Congruent types				Divergent types			
	Mainstayers	*Temperates*	*Doers*	*Aspirers*	*Empathizers*	*Enthusiasts*	*Nonconventionals*	*Explorers*
States in the south census region	22%	11%	14%	13%	9%	11%	8%	12%

South Atlantic

Maryland has higher than national proportions of the following:
    Mainstayers—24%
    Empathizers—17%
    Doers—14%
    Nonconventionals—12%

Washington, DC, has higher than national proportions of the following:
    Aspirers—85%

Virginia has higher than national proportions of the following:
    Aspirers—42%
    Nonconventionals—23%

West Virginia has higher than national proportions of the following:
    Mainstayers—28%
    Temperates—25%
    Empathizers—22%
    Enthusiasts—13%

North Carolina has higher than national proportions of the following:
    Mainstayers—30%
    Enthusiasts—20%
    Temperates—19%
    Nonconventionals—12%

South Carolina has higher than national proportions of the following:
    Empathizers—24%
    Enthusiasts—20%
    Explorers—20%
    Doers—17%

Florida has higher than national proportions of the following:
    Aspirers—18%
    Enthusiasts—16%
    Doers—16%

East South Central

Kentucky has higher than national proportions of the following:
    Mainstayers—34%
    Temperates—29%
    Doers—26%

Tennessee has higher than national proportions of the following:
  Mainstayers—32%
  Temperates—31%
Alabama has higher than national proportions of the following:
  Mainstayers—68%
Mississippi has higher than national proportions of the following:
  Doers—29%
  Mainstayers—23%
  Explorers—23%
  Temperates—16%

West South Central

Louisiana has higher than national proportions of the following:
  Explorers—21%
  Enthusiasts—19%
  Nonconventionals—12%
Texas has higher than national proportions of the following:
  Maintainers—21%
  Explorers—18%
  Aspirers—17%

	Congruent types				Divergent types			
	Main-stayers	*Tem-perates*	*Doers*	*Aspirers*	*Empa-thizers*	*Enthu-siasts*	*Non-conven-tionals*	*Explor-ers*
States in the west census region	12%	10%	8%	15%	11%	14%	16%	15%

Mountain

Colorado has higher than national proportions of the following:
  Temperates—20%
  Doers—17%
  Explorers—16%

Arizona has higher than national proportions of the following:
- Explorers—32%
- Aspirers—24%
- Doers—17%

Pacific

Washington has higher than national proportions of the following:
- Nonconventionals—35%
- Enthusiasts—15%
- Explorers—1.5%
- Aspirers—13%

California has higher than national proportions of the following:
- Empathizers—16%
- Aspirers—15%
- Nonconventionals—13%
- Explorers—14%

Alaska has higher than national proportions of the following:
- Nonconventionals—23%
- Aspirers—16%
- Empathizers—11%

16

Affinities Among the Types

MATCHMAKING

The psychodynamic system would seem a "natural" means for ensuring that two people are compatible with each other—and it is. Matches (or marriages) made on the basis of compatible types, however, are no guarantee that the match will persist as a good one forever. As the section on psychodynamics by age makes clear, there are likely to be changes in a person's type as he/she ages.

This means of course that natural affinity/compatibility will change as the couple ages. For example, one does not remain an explorer forever, and two well-matched explorers at one stage in their lives may evolve into two distinctly different, other types, with probable different levels of natural affinity.

AFFINITIES AMONG THE EIGHT TYPES

By definition, the greatest affinity between two people will be if they are both the same type—indicated by an asterisk (*) in the following table. Affinities between different types will be at lower levels.

The following table shows the affinity between each of the types compared with all other types. The scale is from 10 to 1, where 10 represents the highest level of natural affinity between the two different types and 1 represents the least. Scores between 10 and 6 suggest that people from those types are likely to get along. Scores between 5 and 1 suggest that people of those types are probably not as likely to.

Natural Affinity Grid

	Congruent types				Divergent types			
	Mainstayers	Temperates	Doers	Aspirers	Empathizers	Enthusiasts	Nonconventionals	Explorers
Congruent types								
Mainstayers	*	8	5	7	8	5	1	2
Temperates	8	*	7	5	5	6	4	6
Doers	5	7	*	7	7	5	7	10
Aspirers	7	5	7	*	7	7	6	9
Divergent Types								
Empathizers	8	5	7	7	*	5	7	6
Enthusiasts	5	5	4	7	5	*	7	8
Nonconventionals	1	4	7	6	7	7	*	8
Explorers	2	6	10	9	6	8	9	*

A SUMMARY ANALYSIS OF AFFINITIES
BETWEEN THE DIFFERENT TYPES

Mainstayers tend to have the most selective and the most intense affinities. They are likely to get along well with three other types: temperates (8), empathizers (8), and aspirers (7). They will do the least well of all the types with nonconventionals (1) and explorers (2) and, at a much milder level, enthusiasts (5) and doers (5).

Temperates tend to have slightly broader but less intense affinities. They get on with four types: mainstayers (8), doers (7), enthusiasts (6), and explorers (6). They will not do as well with nonconventionals (4), empathizers (5), and aspirers (5).

Doers have relatively broad affinities, one of which is very strong. They are likely to get along with five other types: explorers (10), temperates (7), aspirers (7), empathizers (7), and nonconventionals (7). They have limited affinity with mainstayers (5) and enthusiasts (5).

Aspirers also have relatively broad affinities, although not generally intense. They are likely to get along with explorers (9), mainstayers (7), doers (7), empathizers (7), enthusiasts (7), and nonconventionals (6). They tend to not get along as well with temperates (5).

Empathizers also tend to have not terribly intense affinities. They are likely to get along with mainstayers (8), doers (7), aspirers (7), nonconventionals (7), and explorers (6). The types they get along with less well are temperates (5) and enthusiasts (5).

Enthusiasts have positive affinity with explorers (8), nonconventionals (7), doers (7), and aspirers (7). They do not do as well with empathizers (5), temperates (5), mainstayers (5), and doers (4).

Nonconventionals do well with explorers (9), empathizers (7), enthusiasts (7), doers (7), and aspirers (6). They do not do at all well with mainstayers (1) but do somewhat better with temperates (4).

Explorers tend to get along well with nearly every type. They have very high affinity with doers and also do well with aspirers (9), enthusiasts (8), nonconventionals (8), temperates (6), and empathizers (6). They are likely not to get on well with mainstayers (2).

17

How Do I Determine Which Type I Am, and How Do I Meet People of the Same or Compatible Types?

HOW DO I DETERMINE WHICH TYPE I AM?

The precise determination of which values type you are is accomplished only through the use of the Tyler psychodynamics algorithm, which assigns scores for each psychodynamic type for each of the qualifying questions. This algorithm is proprietary and is held confidential by Tyler & Associates.

However, a reasonable approximation of a person's type can be accomplished by the reader by following these rules.

First, read the one-page descriptions of the eight types in the appendix. Read them carefully, noting which type you seem to have most in common with. Do not attempt to shade your responses to be the type you may most wish to be, but make your decisions honestly, taking into account both the favorable and not so favorable tendencies noted in the text.

Then read the chapters describing each of the eight types again to assess which of them you seem to have most in common with. If your self-assessment agrees with what you have learned from the one-page summaries, you will have concluded that you are most probably that type.

MEETING PEOPLE OF THE
SAME OR COMPATIBLE TYPES

Meeting people with whom you are most likely to be compatible can be approached by using the information elsewhere in the book. Your most compatible matches are found in the previous chapter, which details which of the types are closest to your own values type.

Voluminous research by academicians has shown that the best and longest-lasting relationships are between people whose values are the closest. These are not necessarily people whom you are most immediately attracted to on the basis of looks alone. But we know that without values compatibility, a relationship is not likely to be formed, nor is it likely to be long-lasting.

But how do you accomplish meeting people whose values are the closest match to who you are?

WHERE YOU LIVE

Many people feel "out of place" or generally uncomfortable with the values of the place in which they reside. Our research has given us the information on the states where people of the eight types tend to be most concentrated. Check the chapter on geography to see if you are already living in one of the states whose values type patterns include concentrations of your own type. If you are, you probably feel reasonably comfortable with the general values climate in which you reside.

LIFESTYLES AND ACTIVITIES INDICATIVE
OF THE VALUES TYPES

Although not perfectly correlated with value types, each of the chapters on type details the lifestyle activities and pursuits favored by each of the eight types. Once you have determined which values type you are likely to be, you can see which activities are favored by your particular type and others with which you have special affinity.

Then you can research which of the most favored activities are available in your local area and pursue participation/membership in them, according to your own preferences. This will increase your exposure to your own values type and put you into closer contact with people with whom you are likely to be most compatible.

SHARED ENTHUSIASMS FOR ACTIVITIES

The following interests, activities, and hobbies are those that are significantly pursued by each of the pairs of psychodynamic types.

Mainstayers and other types

Mainstayers and temperates
>Time with grandchildren
>Sewing
>Walking for health

Mainstayers and doers
>Home workshop/do it yourself
>Hunting

Mainstayers and aspirers
>None

Mainstayers and empathizers
>Bible/devotional reading
>Walking for health

Mainstayers and enthusiasts
>None

Mainstayers and nonconventionals
>Buying prepackaged entertainment

Mainstayers and explorers
>Sewing
>Buying/renting prepackaged entertainment

Temperates and other types

Temperates and doers
>Hiking and backpacking

Temperates and aspirers
  Jogging/running/fast walking
  Playing a musical instrument
  Self-improvement
Temperates and empathizers
  Home furnishing/decorating
  Raising houseplants
  Walking for health
Temperates and enthusiasts
  None
Temperates and nonconventionals
  None
Temperates and explorers
  Collectibles/collections
  Crafts
  Dieting/weight control
  Hiking/backpacking Home
  Furnishing/decorating
  Raising houseplants
  Jogging/running/fast walking
  Needlework/knitting
  Playing a musical instrument
  Sewing

Doers and other types

Doers and aspirers
  Fine art/antiques
  Flying aircraft
  Playing football
  Science/new technologies
  Target/skeet/trap shooting
Doers and empathizers
  Photography
Doers and enthusiasts
  Archery
  Doing automotive work
  Auto racing

    Driving all-terrain vehicles
    Saltwater fishing
    Flying aircraft
    Hang gliding
    Off-road motorcycling
    Playing racquetball
    Snowmobiling
Doers and nonconventionals
    Archery
    Auto racing
    Off-road motorcycling
Doers and explorers
    Fine art/antiques
    Archery
    Auto racing
    Camping trips
    Driving all-terrain vehicles
    Saltwater fishing
    Flying aircraft
    Playing football
    Playing golf
    Hang gliding
    Hiking/backpacking
    Off-road motorcycling
    Performing in a band/orchestra
    Photography
    Playing racquetball
    Science/new technologies
    Snowmobiling
    Target/skeet/trap shooting
    Wildlife conservation

Aspirers and other types

Aspirers and empathizers
    Avid book reading
    Investing in stocks and bonds

Aspirers and enthusiasts
    Electronics
    Flying aircraft
    Horseback riding
    Real estate investment
    Sail boating
    Traveling outside the United States
    Playing volleyball
    Weightlifting
    Studying/collecting wines
Aspirers and nonconventionals
    Avid book reading
    Horseback riding
Aspirers and explorers
    Fine art/antiques
    Attending cultural events
    Electronics
    Fashion/clothing
    Flying aircraft
    Playing football
    Horseback riding
    Investing in stocks and bonds
    Jogging/running/fast walking
    Physical fitness/exercise
    Playing a musical instrument
    Real estate investment
    Sail boating
    Science fiction
    Science/new technologies
    Target/skeet/trap shooting
    Traveling outside the United States
    Playing volleyball
    Weightlifting
    Studying/collecting wines

Empathizers and other types

Empathizers and enthusiasts
    Aerobics
Empathizers and nonconventionals
    Avid book reading
    Entering sweepstakes
Empathizers and explorers
    Aerobics
    Environmental issues
    Home furnishing/decorating
    Raising houseplants
    Photography

Enthusiasts and other types

Enthusiasts and nonconventionals
    Archery
    Auto racing
    Horseback riding
    Off-road motorcycling
    Buying prepackaged entertainment
Enthusiasts and explorers
    Aerobics
    Archery
    Auto racing
    Playing basketball
    Casino gambling
    Coin/stamp collecting
    Driving all-terrain vehicles
    Electronics
    Saltwater fishing
    Flying aircraft
    Gourmet cooking
    Hang gliding
    Horseback riding
    Ice-skating
    Off-road motorcycling

Studying nation's heritage
Patriotic activities/events
Performing in a theater group
Playing a musical instrument
Power boating
Playing racquetball
Real estate investment
Recreational vehicles
Sail boating
Skin/scuba diving
Snowmobiling
Snow skiing, cross-country and downhill
Playing soccer
Playing softball/baseball
Buying/renting prepackaged entertainment
Playing tennis
Traveling outside the United States
Playing volleyball
Water skiing
Weightlifting
Studying/collecting wines

Nonconventionals and other types

Nonconventionals and explorers
  Archery
  Auto racing
  Horseback riding
  Off-road and street motorcycling
  Buying/renting prepackaged entertainment

Explorers and other types

(Already covered in earlier paragraphs)

18

Psychodynamics in Marketing and Advertising

SOME PSYCHODYNAMIC APPLICATIONS IN MARKETING AND ADVERTISING

Psychodynamics significantly helps marketers and advertisers better identify, reach, and influence their markets in the following ways:

- Better identify their markets by psychodynamically typing their customers and prospects and determining the desired target profile(s)
- Better reach their markets by evaluating the comparative psychodynamic profiles of potential advertising sites/media and selecting them accordingly
- Better influence their markets by developing and presenting advertising that speaks to their segment(s) most effectively; selecting advertising themes most psychologically and motivationally congruent with target segments; and determining the optimal contexts, settings, language, characters, icons, and so on for the target profiles

Historically, marketers have had several tools that approximate marketing efficiency/success:

Demographics—the study and use of the standard U.S. census variables, used to establish connection/relationship with purchase behavior
> Principal weakness—They don't reveal much about the "why" of purchase behavior.

Attitudes—positive or negative feelings associated with any symbol, phrase, slogan, person, product, institution, ideal, or idea; attitudinal changes are often predictors of behavioral change
> Principal weakness—They don't tell much about the "who" of purchase behavior.

Psychographics—segmentation systems that combine demographics and attitudes in varying ways
> Principal weakness—Combining the two types of variables weakens one's ability to identify the operant influence(s), obscuring both the "who" and the "why" answers.

Psychodynamics segmentation—a new typology that assesses the psychological, emotional, and motivational forces that are operant, especially at the unconscious level
> Principal benefit—can be used in two ways:
> In combination/support of demography
> As a stand-alone system of consumer segmentation
> Principal weakness—to be determined

PREDISPOSITIONS TO SEEK AND BE RECEPTIVE TO NEW INFORMATION AND EXPERIENCE

Emphasis on the new and innovative versus the old and familiar should be tailored to the predilections of the various psychodynamic types in the target market profiles.

The types differ substantially in their receptivity to both seeking and being receptive to new information and experience. Advertising and promotional campaigns should be carefully tailored to reflect these predispositions.

Psychodynamics types' predisposition to seek new information/experience

Considerably above average
    Explorers
Somewhat above average
    Temperates
    Doers
Average
    Aspirers
    Empathizers
Somewhat below average
    Enthusiasts
    Nonconventionals
Moderately below average
    Mainstayers

Psychodynamics types' predisposition to be receptive to new information/experience

Considerably above average
    Explorers
Moderately above average
    Temperates
    Empathizers
Somewhat above average
    Aspirers
    Nonconventionals
Somewhat below average
    Doers
Moderately below average
    Enthusiasts
Substantially below average
    Mainstayers

Information Receptivity

Analysis by Psychodynamic Types

	Predisposition to be receptive to new information/ experience	Predisposition to seek new information/ experience
Psychodynamic types		
Congruent types		
Mainstayers	– – –	– –
Temperates	++	+
Doers	–	+
Aspirers	+	Avg.
Divergent types		
Empathizers	++	Avg.
Enthusiasts	– –	–
Nonconventionals	+	–
Explorers	+++	+++

MARKET-ENTRY PROCLIVITIES OF THE PSYCHODYNAMIC TYPES

The marketing literature describes five stages in a market's evolution, from the innovators (those people who are the earliest to purchase a new product), to early adopters, to early majority, to the late majority, and finally to the laggards (the last type to purchase a new product).

The types most likely to be the following:

Innovators: nonconventionals, explorers, doers, and enthusiasts
Early adopters: nonconventionals, doers
Early majority: mainstayers, empathizers
Late majority: mainstayers, empathizers
Laggards: mainstayers, empathizers, and temperates

Innovation Propensity Index by Psychodynamic Types*

Psychodynamic Types	Innovators	Early Adopters	Early Majority	Late Majority	Laggards
Congruent Types					
Mainstayers	69	102	134	166	198
Temperates	102	105	108	110	113
Doers	118	109	100	89	80
Aspirers	97	96	95	93	92
Divergent Types					
Empathizers	77	97	119	139	159
Enthusiasts	114	92	71	50	28
Nonconventionals	138	116	92	70	47
Explorers	118	101	83	65	48

* 100 equals "average," higher numbers mean more of that predisposition, and lower than 100 mean less of that predisposition.

INTERNET PURCHASE BEHAVIOR BY PSYCHODYNAMIC TYPE

At this stage of its development, Internet purchase behavior has pretty much evened out across all psychodynamic types, with all types fairly close to each other in their predisposition to purchase products and services through the Internet. Three of the eight types are still below average in this regard, however.

Above average

Temperates
Explorers

Average

Aspirers
Enthusiasts
Nonconventionals

Below average

Mainstayers
Doers
Empathizers

19

Using the Psychodynamic System in Market Segmentation

In an earlier chapter, we noted that three of the principal responsibilities of marketers and advertisers were to identify, reach, and influence the target markets for their products/services.

Using psychodynamics as applied to makes of automobiles provides the following comprehensive information.

IDENTIFYING THE PRODUCT PSYCHODYNAMICALLY

Automobile make ownership preferences differ strongly by psychodynamic type. Some of the makes favored—and not favored—by the psychodynamic types are as follows:

Mainstayers

Some favored makes—Cadillac, GMC
Some makes not favored—Volkswagen, Subaru

Temperates

Some favored makes—Ford, BMW,
Some makes not favored—Mitsubishi, Saab

Doers

Some favored makes—GMC, Chevrolet
Some makes not favored—Mercedes, BMW

Aspirers

Some favored makes—Chrysler, Mercedes
Some makes not favored—Lincoln, Dodge

Empathizers

Some favored makes—Mitsubishi, Volkswagen
Some makes not favored—BMW, Buick

Enthusiasts

Some favored makes—Acura, Lincoln
Some makes not favored—Chrysler, Toyota

Nonconventionals

Some favored makes—Jeep, Subaru
Some makes not favored—Nissan, Chevrolet

Explorers

Some favored makes—Honda, BMW
Some makes not favored—Jeep, Cadillac

REACHING THE TARGET MARKETS

The media favored by the psychodynamic types differ substantially by preference and frequency of usage. Some of the preferred media attended to more frequently than average are the following:

Mainstayers

Radio—religious programs
Magazines—*Southern Living, Modern Maturity*
Television—*Wheel of Fortune*

Temperates

Magazine—*Modern Maturity*

Doers

Radio—nostalgia, big band, sports, talk shows
Magazines—*Four-Wheeler, Motocross Action, Dirt Bike, Off-Road, 4-Wheel Drive Action, Dirt Rider, Bassmaster, Field and Stream, Sports Afield, Outdoor Life, Southern Outdoors, Southern Saltwater, Consumer Reports, Organic Gardening, Popular Mechanics, Popular Science, Home Mechanix, Boating, Sporting News*
Television—*American Sportsman*, Indy 500, professional golf, professional boxing
Cable television—CNBC, adventure, *The American Experience*, nature specials, *This Old House*

Aspirers

Radio—Black/contemporary music
Magazines—*Car and Driver, Motor Trend, Road and Track, Four Wheeler, Sport Truck, 4-Wheel Drive Action, Business Week, Money, Wall Street Journal, Gourmet, Consumer Reports, Consumer's Digest, USA Weekend, Popular Mechanics, Popular Science, Home Mechanix, Esquire, GQ, Penthouse, Cosmopolitan, Newsweek, U.S. News and World Report, USA Today, Smithsonian, Natural History, Tennis*

Television—*Tonight Show*, NBA playoffs, *Wall Street Week, Washington Week in Review*, Bill Moyers, adventure, *Nightly Business Report, Live From Lincoln Center*

Empathizers

Radio—religious programs
Magazines—*New Yorker, Parade*
Television—*The American Experience, Nightly Business Report, Adam Smith's Money World*

Enthusiasts

Radio—rock music, Black/contemporary music
Magazines—*Playboy, Tennis*
Television—daytime drama, *Tonight Show, Late Show*, professional wrestling, MTV

Nonconventionals

Radio—rock music

Explorers

Radio—rock music, Black/rhythm/blues/soul, new age/soft rock, Black/contemporary music
Magazines—*GQ, Playboy, Cosmopolitan, Time, Newsweek, Rolling Stone, Bicycling, Skin Diver, Ski, Skiing, Inside Sports, Outside, Sport, Sports Illustrated, Runner's World, Sporting News*
Television—The arts/concerts/dance, *Late Show*, NCAA football, NCAA basketball, Summer Olympics, Winter Olympics, NBA basketball, Professional golf, professional hockey, Wimbledon/U.S. Open, Weather Channel, *The Living Planet*

INFLUENCING THE TARGET MARKETS

The most effective messages to be conveyed to the target market segments need to be tailored to the interests and the receptivities of the psychodynamic segments.

As detailed in previous chapters, different psychodynamic types have substantially different attitudes not only in general but also toward cars and driving, as well as the motivational factors underlying their automobile ownership.

Some of the types' most distinct automotive-related motivational concepts and messages are as follows.

Mainstayers are cautious, moderate-speed drivers, who do not research their car purchases and tend to buy American makes. High performance does not excite them, and they prefer tried and proven technology and features.

Temperates are nonassertive drivers who worry about safety, reliability, and dependability. High performance does not excite them and ease of service availability is very important to them. They do not consider their cars as extensions of their personality. They object to buying foreign makes, especially Japanese cars.

Doers are very knowledgeable about vehicles and are vehicle enthusiasts—vehicles are the subject of much conversation. They like to tinker with their vehicles themselves to keep them running right.

Aspirers like to be the first to own vehicles new to the market. Hot performance excites them, and they like vehicles that make them the center of attention. Japanese makes are perfectly acceptable to them.

Empathizers tend to purchase base-model vehicles. Reliability is the key—fun with the vehicle is not an issue. They feel little personal involvement or identification with their vehicles and other people and are not knowledgeable about vehicles. They would just as soon buy used as new.

Enthusiasts like vehicles that call attention to themselves. They consider vehicles as indicators of social status, personality, and individuality. They prefer vehicles that are new to the market—unique and innovative, both technologically and from a styling standpoint. They have high levels of loyalty to specific makes and like the feeling of power a high driver's perch provides.

Nonconventionals feel less connected and less involved with their vehicles. They tend to buy base-model vehicles with minimal equipment and do not maintain their vehicles well or with enthusiasm. They have little interest in buying American makes and have high levels of loyalty to specific makes.

Explorers like vehicles that call attention to themselves and consider vehicles important ways of expressing their personality and individuality. They are fast and aggressive drivers and want high levels of power, speed, and performance. They will buy nondomestic makes in preference to American makes.

20

Political Outlook and Party Financial Support

The political outlook among the psychodynamic types varies considerably. Majorities, or near majorities, of four of the types describe themselves as having a conservative viewpoint—mainstayers (54%), temperates (52%), doers (54%), and aspirers (46%). Strong pluralities (at least) describe themselves as "middle-of-the-roaders" rather than either conservative or liberal. Fewer than 3 in 10 of 6 of the types describe themselves as having a liberal outlook.

All types except explorers lean more toward the conservative viewpoint rather than toward the liberal viewpoint. Explorers are the only type that lean more toward the liberal point of view than the conservative—but by just a shade.

However, when it comes to donating to one or another of the major political parties, majorities of five of the types have donated to the Democratic Party—mainstayers (50%), doers (88%), aspirers (53%), empathizers (60%), and explorers (79%), while majorities of four types have donated to the Republican Party—mainstayers (50%), temperates (71%), enthusiasts (57%), and nonconventionals (88%). (An equal majority [50%] of mainstayers have donated to both parties.)

Psychodynamic Types—Percentage Distributions by Political Outlook—Percentages Read Down

Political outlook cohorts	Congruent types				Divergent types			
	Main-stayers	Temperates	Doers	Aspirers	Empa-thizers	Enthusiasts	Noncon-ventionals	Explorers
Very conservative	16	9	12	10	8	6	6	5
Somewhat conservative	38	43	42	36	27	25	30	22
Middle of the road	35	34	40	34	38	55	50	43
Somewhat liberal	10	14	6	15	18	13	14	28
Very liberal	1	1	1	5	9	2	1	3

Psychodynamic Types—Percentage Distributions by Political Party Monetary Support

Have donated to one of the two major, national political parties	Congruent types				Divergent types			
	Main-stayers	Temperates	Doers	Aspirers	Empa-thizers	Enthusiasts	Noncon-ventionals	Explorers
Democratic Party	50	29	88	53	60	43	13	79
Republican Party	50	71	13	47	40	57	88	21

One-Page Summaries of the Eight Psychodynamic Types

MAINSTAYERS—20% of the Population

Personal/Societal Affinities
Personal contentment/happiness with one's self—average
Believe in treating others fairly/ethically—above average
Affinity with local area/community—high
Affinity with country—high
Affinity with the global community—low

A Brief Psychological/Motivational Profile
Mainstayers are loyal, patriotic people with a strong nationalistic bent. They have fervent spiritual, moral affiliations; like patriotic events; and want a strong military. Their aim is to belong and fit in; their focus is on their families, homes, communities, and country. Their preference is for the known and the predictable. They are frequently devout members of mainstream religions.

Religious and Spiritual Differences From the "Average" Portrait
Alone among the eight types, majorities of mainstayers do not believe that every religion is equally valid in the eyes of God; someone can be a good person without believing in God. Many consider themselves born-again Christians (along with many temperates).

Some Words and Phrases to Help in Visualizing Mainstayers
Quiet evenings at home, fitting in, doing what is right, playing by the rules, watching television, patriotic, maintain a strong military, like parades, support economic protectionism, community events, resistant to change, volunteer fire department, Boy Scouts and Girl Scouts, criminals get too much coddling, flag burners should go to jail, hard to convince, see American first, buy American, brand loyal, have little trust in government or big business.

Personal Traits Frequently Respected by Others
Strongly value the concept of law and consider it highly important to follow/play by the rules.

Personal Traits Not Universally Loved by Others
Can be intolerant of people outside of the American cultural mainstream or with differing belief systems.

Political Leanings
Tend toward the conservative. Equally likely to support the Democratic or Republican Party.

Some Favored Activities and Lifestyles
Traveling in the United States, walking for health, home workshop/do it yourself, gardening, time with grandchildren, crafts, bible/devotional reading, hunting, buying/renting prerecorded videos.

Types With Whom They Have Positive Affinity
Other mainstayers and temperates.

TEMPERATES—11% of the Population

Personal/Societal Affinities
Personal contentment/happiness with one's self—average
Believe in treating others fairly/ethically—high
Affinity with local area/community—above average
Affinity with country—high
Affinity with the global community—below average

A Brief Psychological/Motivational Profile
Temperates hold strong nonmaterialistic values. They believe that money, possessions, and position are not indicators of real success in life. They are highly disposed to follow their country's laws, customs, and mores. They reject extravagance. They are strong supporters of the American culture, American workers, and American products. They tend to live according to their own strong sense of spirituality and morality. Their vocational emphasis is on doing something well that they enjoy.

Religious and Spiritual Differences From the "Average" Portrait
Many, along with mainstayers, consider themselves to be born-again Christians.

Some Words and Phrases to Help in Visualizing Temperates
Nonmaterialistic, frugal, focus on simplification, believe the job is more important than the money, reject extravagance, not impulsive, success in life and possessions are not the same thing, content with the status quo, simple pleasures, like to watch television, not avid readers, support America, buy American, like the outdoors, never spend more than what is needed, treat people fairly, never take unfair advantage.

Personal Traits Frequently Respected by Others
Try to be staunch practitioners of the Golden Rule in their everyday dealings with others.

Personal Traits Not Universally Loved by Others
Can be intolerant of people with differing belief systems.

Political Leanings
Tend toward the conservative. More likely to support the Republican Party.

Some Favored Activities and Lifestyles
Gardening, walking for health, home furnishing/decorating, jogging/running, freshwater fishing, raising houseplants, crafts, dieting, self-improvement, performing in a band/orchestra, avid book reading, time with grandchildren, needlework/knitting, sewing, wildlife conservation, collectibles, hiking, bible/devotional reading, patriotic events.

Types With Whom They Have Positive Affinity
Other temperates, mainstayers, doers, enthusiasts, and explorers.

DOERS—12% of the Population

Personal/Societal Affinities
Personal contentment/happiness with one's self—average
Believe in treating others fairly/ethically—average
Affinity with local area/community—average
Affinity with country—above average
Affinity with the global community—below average

A Brief Psychological/Motivational Profile
Doers believe in following their country's laws and mores. They are down-to-earth, sensible, and practical people whose principal focus, talents, and preoccupations are in the hands-on doing of things. Their orientation is toward the pragmatic accomplishment of specific tasks. Either by vocation or by temperament, they are people who like to build, make, or fix things. They are skilled with manipulating and interacting with all sorts of tools, machinery, and equipment. They love and strongly prefer the outdoors.

Religious and Spiritual Differences From the "Average" Portrait
They are less inclined to agree that living in accordance with their religious beliefs is very important to them and that their moral standards are higher than most people's.

Some Words and Phrases to Help in Visualizing Doers
Like tools; like working with their hands; do-it-yourselfers; like to build, fix, and repair things other people wouldn't tackle; competitive; like roughing it; extreme conditions; like mechanical things; like taking things apart; like planning projects; not squeamish; like hardware stores; can never have too many tools; don't mind getting dirty; like fishing, hunting, and so on; like motorized vehicles of all types; like weapons; are happiest when something in the household breaks down and they get to fix it.

Personal Traits Frequently Respected by Others
Are highly valued as friends and neighbors because of their practical talents and their love of being able to do things that others are impressed by and find helpful.

Personal Traits Not Universally Loved by Others
Can be nonpolitically correct in their beliefs concerning the appropriate societal roles for women.

Political Leanings
Tend to be conservative or middle of the road. Strongly support the Democratic Party.

Some Favored Activities and Lifestyles
Home workshop, camping, hunting, fishing, weapons, automotive work, all strenuous outdoor activities, television sports.

Types With Whom They Have Positive Affinity
Other doers, explorers, temperates, aspirers, empathizers, and nonconventionals.

ASPIRERS—12% of the Population

Personal/Societal Affinities
Personal contentment/happiness with one's self—average
Believe in treating others fairly/ethically—below average
Affinity with local area/community—average
Affinity with country—average
Affinity with the global community—average

A Brief Psychological/Motivational Profile
The main drive of the aspirers is in striving toward and measuring up to those criteria that they consider to represent the highest in personal standards. Their principal goals include personal success, personal recognition, achieving high status, making a good appearance, and making a good impression. They are highly competitive and seek to distinguish themselves from others by virtue of superiority in morals, personal standards, physical condition, dress, and the quantity and quality of their possessions. They are predisposed to follow society's prevailing laws and mores.

Religious and Spiritual Differences From the "Average" Portrait
They are more likely to agree that someone can be a good person without believing in God, and their moral standards are higher than most other people's.

Some Words and Phrases to Help in Visualizing Aspirers
Focus on achievement, high standards, only the best, right to the top, measure up, stay in shape, dress well, self-improvement, appearances are important, make a good impression, status counts, look important, status symbols, clothes make the man/woman, set themselves apart, competitive, energetic, self-satisfied, associate with/emulate important people, be the best you can be, avoid/do not associate with ordinary things/people.

Personal Traits Frequently Respected by Others
Hold themselves to high personal standards.

Personal Traits Not Universally Loved by Others
Can behave as though they were superior to other people and entitled to greater consideration and status.

Political Leanings
Lean conservative or middle of the road. Tend slightly toward Democratic Party.

Some Favored Activities and Lifestyles
Physical fitness, watching sports on television, jogging, buying/renting DVDs, self-improvement, home furnishing, fashion, avid book reading, weightlifting, camping, shooting.

Types With Whom They Have Positive Affinity
Other aspirers, explorers, mainstayers, doers, empathizers, enthusiasts, and nonconventionals.

EMPATHIZERS—10% of the Population

Personal/Societal Affinities
Personal contentment/happiness with one's self—average
Believe in treating others fairly/ethically—average
Affinity with local area/community—average
Affinity with country—below average
Affinity with the global community—very high

A Brief Psychological/Motivational Profile
Empathizers have a broad perspective and field of vision. They are attuned and sensitive to the needs and concerns of others, irrespective of where they are or what country they live in. They do not have a strong sense of nationalism and tend to believe that nationalism stands in the way of humankind's highest aspirations, potential, and achievements. They are distrustful of the motives of political and economic leaders and skeptical of their motives toward and connectedness with the "universal good," fair play, and the needs and rights of society at large. Their sensitivities and concerns extend to animals as well as to people.

Religious and Spiritual Differences From the "Average" Portrait
Empathizers have no meaningful differences.

Some Words and Phrases to Help in Visualizing Empathizers
Think globally, personal sacrifice for the universal good, save our planet, animal rights, nationalism does not work, challenge authority, environmental issues, share the earth's resources more equitably, the good of all humankind, skepticism of governmental leaders, skepticism of big business.

Personal Traits Frequently Respected by Others
Have a highly sensitive and concerned perspective that encompasses all peoples and all species.

Personal Traits Not Universally Loved by Others
When their country's national interests conflict with the world community's interests, they may well tend toward the world's side of those arguments.

Political Leanings
More middle of the road than conservative or liberal. More strongly supportive of the Democratic than the Republican Party.

Some Favored Activities and Lifestyles
Traveling inside and outside the United States, walking for health, avid book reading, home furnishing/decorating, environmental issues, bible/devotional reading, photography, raising houseplants, dieting, aerobics, saltwater fishing, collectibles, fashion.

Types With Whom They Have Positive Affinity
Other empathizers, mainstayers, doers, aspirers, nonconventionals, and explorers.

ENTHUSIASTS—11% of the Population

Personal/Societal Affinities

Personal contentment/happiness with one's self—very low
Believe in treating others fairly/ethically—very low
Affinity with local area/community—low
Affinity with country—below average
Affinity with the global community—average

A Brief Psychological/Motivational Profile

Enthusiasts are oriented toward the getting and the doing of the things that they believe make life worthwhile. They are materialistic and pursue what they consider to be life's pleasures. They like money and enjoy spending it to get and have the best of what it is that they want. They tend to be impatient with things that stand in the way of these goals and will bend rules and regulations that they find inconvenient. Their principal focus is toward self-gratification. They support the country's economic system, foreign policies, products, ideas, and philosophies. They believe that their country's interests take precedence over the interests of the world community.

Religious and Spiritual Differences From the "Average" Portrait

Enthusiasts are likely to agree that someone can be a good person without believing in God.

Some Words and Phrases to Help in Visualizing Enthusiasts

Focus on getting and having what they want, materialistic, impulsive, extravagant, pay what it takes to get what they want, pleasure-focused, luxuries make life worthwhile.

Personal Traits Frequently Respected by Others

Love excitement and can be extravagant in the entertaining and pleasing of others.

Personal Traits Not Universally Loved by Others

May well behave as though it were appropriate to take unfair advantage of others.

Political Leanings

Strongly middle of the road with a slightly conservative bent. More likely to support the Republican Party.

Some Favored Activities and Lifestyles

Live on the edge, activities with strong elements of risk or danger, gamble, excitement, always looking for activities and events that offer new thrills, actively pursue virtually all outdoor and indoor sports and games, casino gambling, skiing, snowmobiling, all-terrain vehicles, collecting wines, real estate investment, traveling outside the United States. Second only to explorers in the incidence and frequency of activities pursued.

Types With Whom They Have Positive Affinity

Other enthusiasts, explorers, nonconventionals, doers, and aspirers.

NONCONVENTIONALS—11% of the Population

Personal/Societal Affinities
Personal contentment/happiness with one's self—below average
Believe in treating others fairly/ethically—low
Affinity with local area/community—below average
Affinity with country—low
Affinity with the global community—average

A Brief Psychological/Motivational Profile
Nonconventionals tend to operate outside of society's "mainstream." They are impatient and will bend or break the rules to do or to get what they want. They have little sympathy with the established order of things. Nonconventionals tend to have a "live and let live" philosophy, to be permissive and self-indulgent, and to stretch the bounds of convention. They place little value on playing by the rules. They are very tolerant of other people who are similarly out of the mainstream.

Religious and Spiritual Differences From the "Average" Portrait
Nonconventionals are less likely to agree that the world literally was created in 6 days, that living in accordance with their religious/spiritual beliefs is very important to them, that they are born-again Christians, and that their moral standards are higher than most other people's. They are more likely to agree that every religion is equally valid in the eyes of God and that someone can be a good person without believing in God.

Some Words and Phrases to Help in Visualizing Nonconventionals
Offbeat, unconventional, freethinkers, originals, breaking the mold, fad starters, countercultural, outrageous dress/style/cosmetics, out-of-the-box thinking.

Personal Traits Frequently Respected by Others
Tend to have a "live and let live" philosophy and to be very tolerant of other people's belief systems and of people out of the cultural mainstream.

Personal Traits Not Universally Loved by Others
May well not "play by the rules" and may disregard the culture's current ethic in achieving what they want.

Political Leanings
Tend to be "middle-of-the-roaders" with a conservative bent. Strongly support the Republican Party.

Some Favored Activities and Lifestyles
Parties, alcoholic beverages and other mood-altering substances, taking up new activities, off-road vehicles, motorcycling, hang gliding, entering sweepstakes, avid book reading, weapons of all types.

Types With Whom They Have Positive Affinity
Other nonconventionals, explorers, empathizers, enthusiasts, doers, and aspirers.

EXPLORERS—13% of the Population

Personal/Societal Affinities

Personal contentment/happiness with one's self—average
Believe in treating others fairly/ethically—average
Affinity with local area/community—below average
Affinity with country—average
Affinity with the global community—above average

A Brief Psychological/Motivational Profile

Explorers are active, energetic, and extroverted people who like to "push the envelope." They are always among the first to try new experiences, activities, and sports, especially physically demanding ones that offer the prospect of risk, excitement, and new thrills. They seek the limelight and love to entertain. They love change just for variety. They are often trendsetters. They have few qualms about bending or breaking the existing rules. They have strong interest in experiencing other countries and cultures.

Religious and Spiritual Differences From the "Average" Portrait

Explorers tend to disagree that the world literally was created in 6 days. They tend not to be born-again Christians. They are more likely to agree that someone can be a good person without believing in God and believe their moral standards are higher than most other people's.

Some Words and Phrases to Help in Visualizing Explorers

Sports minded, active, competitive, energetic, adventuresome, experimental, talkative, love excitement, new thrills, showing off, let's party, let's play, don't stay home, vital, vigorous, open minded, bold, unafraid, love a challenge, risk, exhibitionistic.

Personal Traits Frequently Respected by Others

Are people whose energies, enthusiasms, interests, ideas, and charisma can be appealing and contagious to others in their orbit; very tolerant of many types of other people.

Personal Traits Not Universally Loved by Others

May not "play by the rules" and may disregard the current cultural ethic in their behaviors and attitudes.

Political Leanings

Middle of the road. Slightly more likely to lean liberal than conservative.

Some Favored Activities and Lifestyles

The highest ranking of the eight types in the incidence and frequency of participation in virtually all of the activities and lifestyles measured, including new, cutting edge sports; all standard sports; all traveling; all outdoor activities (in all seasons); performing arts; all motorized vehicles; gambling; exercise; home improvement; investing.

Types With Whom They Have Positive Affinity

Other explorers, doers, aspirers, enthusiasts, nonconventionals, temperates, and empathizers.

John M. (Jack) Tyler

A Brief Biography

Education

AB in English—Franklin & Marshall
MS in Psychology—Rutgers

Work History

Vice President—Opinion Research Corporation, Princeton, NJ
  CEO of Western Operations, heading up offices in San Francisco
  and Los Angeles
Director of Custom Research, as well as Director of Marketing, for
 SRI's (Stanford Research Institute's) Values and Lifestyles (VALS)
 Psychographics Program
Founder and President, Tyler & Associates
  Specializing in market segmentation and consumer psychology
  Expert in psychographics
  Developer of the Psychodynamics segmentation system

Contact information:

ADDRESS: PO Box 344
   Corte Madera, CA 94976
EMAIL: tylberg@comcast.net
WEBSITE: Psychodynamics.com